immersed in the sacred

immersed in the sacred

discovering the "small s" sacraments

kathy coffey

ave maria press   Notre Dame, Indiana

www.avemariapress.com

International Standard Book Number: 0-87793-962-4

Cover and text design by Katherine Robinson Coleman

Printed and bound in the United States of America.

Library of Congress Cataloging-in-Publication Data

Coffey, Kathy.

Immersed in the sacred : discovering the "small s" sacraments / Kathy Coffey.

   p. cm.

Includes bibliographical references (p.   ).

ISBN 0-87793-962-4

   1. Sacraments. I. Title.

BV800 .C59 2003

242--dc21

                                                        2002152565

                                                              CIP

For my "sisters"—bound not by blood, but by love:

Trish Dunn

Mary Ann Figlino, C.S.J.

Anne Flood, S.C.

Kathy Fortune

LaVonne Neff

You make of my days a sacrament.

Contents

Introduction

Sometimes when we are still and alone, we sense a yearning so deep it aches. "This life is sometimes pleasant, sometimes painful," says the quiet inner voice. "Isn't there more to it than ups and downs?"

This search for something "more than meets the eye" is everyone's. We all want fuller, richer lives, in which we can sometimes feel something more than human, something like the presence of God. In the midst of chaos and commotion, anxiety and sadness, we grope for the sacred that undergirds or overreaches the ordinary experience. Besieged by the negative, we yearn for something positive.

We want to appreciate *now* what Emily in *Our Town* saw only after her death. Returning to earth and revisiting her twelfth birthday, she realized that "Grover's Corners . . . Mama and Papa . . . clocks ticking and Mama's sunflowers . . . food and coffee . . . new-ironed dresses and hot baths . . . and sleeping and waking up" are treasures "too wonderful for anybody to realize." Emily asks, "Do any human beings ever realize life while they live it—every, every minute?" The stage manager responds, "The saints and poets, maybe—they do some."

Emily names places, people, activities, and objects that enrich life on earth. Some would even say that these communicate God's presence in this world. If a human being simply says he or she loves another, we may be skeptical. But if that person's love takes on the shape of deeds—visible, concrete actions like a late-night run to the grocery store—the words are more convincing. So, too, God's love for humanity must take a shape that we can understand: the tangible places, people, activities, and objects that fill our days.

If we begin to decode God's communication, then we know that the sacred hides in the stuff of our lives; the holy does not inhabit a distant realm beyond us. We can find meaning in the dreariest day if we only know where to look. In this quest, a tradition that has always found significance in the ordinary may be especially helpful. It is the tradition of *sacrament.*

The notion of sacrament depends on the idea that God can be found in this world, indeed, that this world shouts of the sacred. "All of creation is an immense sacrament. All created things are signs of God that we decipher in order to find our way to God."[1]

The History of Sacrament

Since the concept of sacrament is basic here, let's explore a brief history of the word. For centuries, people have found satisfaction for their deepest longing in their ordinary human experiences. Through the gestures of bathing, anointing, feeding, reconciling, marrying, committing to service, and embracing the sick or dying, they have found a meeting of the deeply human and the divine.

"Sacramental thinking and practice is rooted in the human condition, and has many important parallels with human ritual life in other cultures."[2] Every culture has its sacred places, people, actions, and objects. Hindus bathe in the Ganges, Jews eat a Passover meal, Muslims go on pilgrimage to Mecca, Buddhists honor their monks, Polynesians dance, and Christians revere the cross. Each symbol points beyond itself, to something mysterious and holy.[3]

The specifically Christian history of sacrament stretches back to a Roman temple. Picture that scene: a shadowy interior after the brash color and heat of the marketplace, cool marble, shades of blue-gray, a hush. As eyes adjust to the dimness, lean against a pillar and survey the scene.

Two people enter the temple; much as we'd like to make this gender-inclusive, they are probably both men—who, after all, conducted the business in the Roman Empire. They lay on the altar a pledge: each one carefully stacks there a large sum of money. Their words are cursory; they agree that whoever breaks their contract forfeits the sum. Or, the winner of a suit collects the whole sum. That pledge—the money, the goods—is called a *sacramentum*. In a sacred space, it symbolizes more than the object itself.

Later the word *sacramentum* came to mean a soldier's oath of allegiance to a commander and the gods. Later still, Christians applied the term to their ceremony of initiation, in which a convert expressed allegiance to God and the new community. By the fifth century, St. Augustine defined *sacramentum* as "a sign of a sacred reality." Most essential for this book, he declared: "there is nothing that cannot become a sacramental encounter." In this universal sense, any person, place, or thing can be a symbol of the mysterious sacred. "And if sacraments are understood in this broader sense, then the religions of the world are full of sacraments."[4]

It is that "broader sense" of sacrament to which we'll return. But as time went on, usage of the word became more restricted. By the twelfth century, Catholics used the word to refer only to seven rituals which occurred mostly in church: baptism, confirmation, eucharist, reconciliation, marriage, ordination, and the sacrament of the sick. Medieval theologians thought about sacraments in a highly sophisticated way, but they focused more on their function than on their roots in human experience.[5] By the sixteenth century the word was further restricted by Protestants who reduced the number of sacraments to fewer than seven, and in many cases, the two with a clear biblical basis: baptism and eucharist.

As the meaning of the word narrowed, the relationship between church sacrament and lived experience was de-emphasized. When people "fixed" the sacraments in certain official forms, they began to forget that the sacred could appear in new or surprising places. Restricting the sacraments to the brief moment of celebration diminishes their link "to an ongoing process of recognizing God's presence in all of life."[6]

Some argue that formal religion has not kept pace with contemporary developments and has failed to address people's deepest yearnings. They caution that a concentration on the priestly role in sacramental celebration can turn everyone else into passive spectators. Rules and repetition can drain away the original poetry. What was once filled with mystery and grace can become a mechanism for salvation confined within church walls.

Robert Hovda puts it metaphorically: "We had it all explained, overexplained, in blueprints and production charts. You pulled the levers right and you hit the jackpot every time." But more profound hungers went unfilled. "The satisfactory trade relations we had established with the Almighty turned out—in the stress of living—to be something less than the stuff of commitment and of meaning."[7]

The Small s Sacraments

Left with unsatisfied hunger, where do we go? We know that the all-powerful and all-present God is not held captive within the walls of a church building. Surely God seeks people where we are, as we are, and touches us in ways that communicate personally. People, places, actions, and objects, no matter where we meet them, can be vehicles for grace and entrées to the sacred.

Depending on our traditions, we honor seven or two sacraments as special channels of grace. But we cannot fully appreciate those unless we also look for other markers of God's presence throughout our experience. The church sacraments that revere certain persons, places, actions, and objects as God's communication lead us beyond them to more: what we might call the *sacraments of the world*. In this book, these are called the "small s" sacraments. They refer to all creation, where we seek a satisfaction of the thirst for God that is our deepest longing.

The work of Andrew Greeley has already identified the "sacramental imagination," which finds God lurking everywhere. As St. Augustine said, "If you have an eye for it, the world itself is a sacrament." But the question remains: How, specifically, do we live a life permeated by such a vision? While respecting the sacraments celebrated in church, how do we also find the holy in the office, home, garage, or shop?

What follows is one person's answer, one attempt to broaden the definition of sacrament to include the lowercase as well as uppercase—or return to Augustine's large, inclusive view. The pattern of each section begins with some familiar sacramental symbols, revered for centuries. Seeing how *some* places, people, objects, and activities were uplifted and designated sacred, and still holding these special, we can apply that process to others. Then perhaps we can recognize a richness flowing from the rituals of the church into more sacraments than we ever dreamed. If we are, in fact, surrounded by sacraments, their buoyant presence might address our persistent ache for something more.

The perspective set forth here is admittedly shaped by Catholic heritage, middle-class lifestyle, a feminine perspective, and personal quirks. But the quest it describes transcends denominational boundaries and opens a way to all seekers who want to deepen their ordinary experience.

For it is, above all, a walk in grace. As with any narrative, we look for the resonances between a book and our own lives, seek wedges of understanding, try to make a "fit" between words on a page and where we are right now. In doing so, we find we are not alone. Our longings—and their satisfactions—are similar because of our shared humanity.

So let's begin with a reflection that links sacraments and daily life, a process of connecting that recurs throughout this book. Read it slowly and meditatively, inserting your own thoughts at the prompts.

A Meditation on Sacraments and Daily Life

After a long, hot walk or ride through a dusty landscape, we plunge our hands and faces into water, grab a drink, or jump into a shower, the urge for cleansing water so basic we may not even think about it.

Remember a recent experience with water . . .

After that bath, we spread some silken lotion on the skin. Or, a sunburn aches or a wound festers. We soothe it with ointment. Instinctively, we care for the skin that is the human envelope, that protects us from and presents us to the world. And if the oil is rich and fragrant, so much the better!

Remember a recent experience with lotion or oil . . .

After an unusually hectic day, we remember that we have not eaten. Lunch and maybe even breakfast got lost in a rush of activity. And suddenly, we have Major Hunger. For the moment, nothing seems as satisfying as digging into the bagel, the hamburger, the dinner.

Remember a recent, special meal . . .

After a long estrangement, we see the friend or relative who was dear to us. The original cause of

14

disagreement seems obscure; in a rush we remember only that person's finest points. Words come in a torrent, or suddenly, we embrace. All that divided us is forgotten; all that hurt us is forgiven. Reconnecting with this person, we also discover some part of ourselves that had been lost.

Remember a recent reconciliation . . .

Finally we meet one who seems like ourselves, we see the glimmer of a soul mate or best friend, and want to spend a long time together. We want to be with that person, and that person alone, for a lifetime. So we gather ourselves together and in one sweeping gesture, commit all that we are in love and hope.

Remember a commitment you made in love . . .

The young woman with her new MBA or the recently retired grandpa commits two years to the Peace Corps. The mom drives the umpteenth carpool; the dad gets up with the sick child in the middle of the night. A social worker stays overtime; an attorney takes on another pro bono case. They all commit to serve something beyond themselves; their own interests are set aside for another's.

Remember a recent experience of service,
your own or another's . . .

A body that was long familiar and beloved grows emaciated and weak. The life seems to ebb from one we want to hold close. And so we must be near the person, rubbing a back, touching a hand, offering comfort or medicine, doing anything we can to reassure, to remind them what a treasure they are and have always been to us. We do not want to let them go, but at the same time, we bless their going.

Remember the illness or dying of a loved one . . .

PART ONE

Places as Sanctuaries

Native Americans are among the many ancient peoples who set aside certain places as sacred. The Bible is also firmly anchored in a sense of place. Recall, for instance, the visit of angels to Abraham and Sarah's tent, Moses on the mountain, or Jesus in the Garden of Olives and know that these are privileged places where people meet God. While some encounters with the divine occur in churches, many happen in houses or are swept by the clean winds of the outdoors.

As we remember our own encounters with God, we are like the artist drawn to a particular slant of light on city, desert, or coast. The meeting transforms an ordinary place into a sanctuary, whether it's a mountain or garden, hotel or home. While our experiences may not be as dramatic as the transfiguration, we can understand Peter's desire to set up tents and stay on the mountaintop. Yet Jesus led them back down. He believed that "the back roads of Galilee and the innermost sanctuary of the Temple were equally holy places. . . ."[1]

Many writers have explored the direct links between outer and inner geography. Belden Lane describes the "enormous energy that landscape metaphors exert on the human imagination."[2] Thomas Merton adds: "It is essential to experience all the times and moods of one good place. No one will ever be able to say how essential, how truly part of a genuine life this is: but all this is lost in the abstract, formal routine of exercises under an official fluorescent light."[3]

As you read this section, be sensitive to the question:

In what places do you feel God's presence?

Then spend some time in reflection or discussion about those places that are sacred to you.

Gazebo:
Place of Reconciliation

Out beyond ideas of wrongdoing and rightdoing, there is a field. I'll meet you there.[4]

—*Rumi*

The only door we have to the absolute, the only bridge to the sacred begins in this world, opens through concrete and specific places. So our memories are tethered to locations: the church where I made first communion, the restaurant where we got engaged, the hospital where our children were born, the cemetery where my brother is buried, the vacation spot where we always relax.

In a workshop on family spirituality, I often ask participants to diagram their homes. This is a quick draw, not a precise architectural floor plan. Then I ask them to label with a "B" the places where they experience echoes of baptism (usually these are places where cleansing occurs: the bathroom, the laundry room). They do the same for eucharist (kitchen or dining room), marriage or commitment (not only the bedroom!), the sacrament of the sick, and reconciliation.

Finally, they look at their completed diagrams and reflect on two Bible verses: "In my Father's house there are many dwelling places" (Jn 14:2) and "You are a royal priesthood, a holy nation, God's own people" (1 Pt 2:9). The comments that follow are often insightful: "I didn't realize how sacramental we are!" or "*Every* room is sacred space." One lady mused, "I marked R for Reconciliation all over the place, because we goof up everywhere!"

I agreed with her mightily, but I thought especially about another place that for me is the locus of reconciliation. As many people know, I am fanatically attached to a Jesuit retreat center about forty-five minutes from my home. Its modest buildings are set on 300 acres of spectacular scenery in the foothills of the Rocky Mountains. As I turn off the highway and onto its drive, my blood pressure drops significantly.

My ritual on arrival there is always the same: use the bathroom, grab a cup of coffee, and walk west to the gazebo. It stands on an isolated point overlooking the whole front range. In different seasons and at different times of day, the colors and textures of the panorama change. But always to the west is the sweep from Long's Peak on the northern horizon to Pike's Peak in the south. To the east, a swath of prairie is crosshatched by train tracks. If a place can have a theme, a friend once named it, looking west: "the desire of the everlasting hills."

The gazebo is a simple wood structure, open on all sides, containing only a few chairs. A chain ropes off the doorway to discourage wandering cows. Birds nest in the overhead beams; grasses and wildflowers grow around the base. The dark prongs of a rabbit's ears might be silhouetted in the underbrush; in the fall the scrub oak glows orange. I have always loved the poet Rumi's line: "The soul is here for its own joy." But in the gazebo, I accent it differently: "The soul is *here* for its own joy."

This is where the important work of mending goes on after a long absence. In the course of a retreat, I may read, hike, have inspiring conversations with my spiritual director, pray the liturgy, and rest. But finally all the reading, journaling, walking, and talking comes to a halt. Here I stop everything. I sit alone in the deep peace of the gazebo, but I am not really alone. Within, I hear a voice that can only be God's because the tone of light mockery is uncharacteristic of my serious self: "Did you think I wouldn't come?"

The first reconciliation, then, is with God. How often I have failed to trust, worrying about numerous details which God all along was handling. The fretting and stewing often led to an "ah ha" moment when everything worked out, or didn't, but I survived. Knowing that God is intimately involved in even the minutiae of our lives gives us unshakable confidence— but we forget it too often. Remembering is the first step inching toward reconciliation.

The second step is to mentally hold close my family and friends, many people who are dear. How often I have brushed them off under the pressure of a tight schedule or a deadline. Sometimes all they needed was a minute of courtesy or attention, and I was too dumb to see the need. When other people give so much, it is downright embarrassing to see how little I reciprocate. So I think of them lovingly now, holding them in my heart, lifting them to God's. It is a small thing, hardly compensating for the neglect, but it is the start toward restored relationships.

The third step, peacemaking, comes with the self. Most humans house multiple voices; the trick is helping the chorus to harmonize. I learned long ago that as an introvert, I need lots of time for inner and outer selves to chat, for desires and demands to get friendly, for the whole crazy cacophony to simmer down and be still. Without this inner harmony, I'm not much use to anyone.

Furthermore, I need to regularly pop the bubble of the satisfied self. The "I'm doing just fine, thank you" side of the personality likes to gloss over the difficulties and sail through genuine evil. Our arrogance refuses to admit how wormy, deceitful, smarmy, and outrageous we can sometimes be. It's probably not healthy to dwell on our warts all the time. But in the stillness of the gazebo where all is admitted, all is forgiven.

It is not a place for visions, raptures, or grandiose annunciations. Whatever insights come make a difficult entrance past all the defensive mechanisms usually erected for self-protection. In our arrogance, we tend to glide along on accomplishments, ears attuned to the applause. We never calculate what our success might cost others, or admit how broken and incomplete we really are. In the silence of the place comes the realization of how little I have, but it is enough.

Andrew Harvey tells another story of "enough," about a pilgrimage in quest of Great Experience. The seeker, however, never arrives at enlightenment in the Tibetan monastery. Instead he is captivated by the beauty along the way and concludes: "to walk by a stream, watching the pebbles darken in the running water, is enough; to sit under the apricots is enough; to sit in a circle of great red rocks, watching them slowly begin to throb and dance as the silence of my mind deepens, is enough."[5]

So sitting in the gazebo, paying attention, examining and quieting myself is as vital as oxygen. As Henri Nouwen points out, "We serve the world by being spiritually well. The first question is not, 'How much do we do?' or 'How many people do we help out?' but 'Are we interiorly at peace?'"[6]

The pathways to peace will differ for each person and each personality type. Some of my friends find it in service, some in their families, others through the arts or animals. While at different times these channels are also fruitful for me, I have learned that many kinds of reconciliation can occur at the gazebo.

Usually driven by the clock, I lose all sense of time here. If we believe, as we say we do, that Christ is alive for us, longing to be with us, wanting to make us into his home, then we must offer him these wide empty times and spaces to do so. He says to us as he did to Zacchaeus, "I must stay at *your house* today" (Lk 19:5).

A mantra for yoga instructors seems to be "listen to your body." In the rare cases when we actually pay attention and focus on it, we are surprised to hear its aches and pains, its energies and rhythms. This must be true when we listen to God whole-heartedly, filtering out other voices. More important than any word I write or talk I give is this listening, deepening time. I will leave here a better person than when I came. This plunge into healing has indeed been sacramental.

As late afternoon breezes drift through the gazebo and the sky fills with the first gauzy pink hints of sunset, I know God is here. More important, I know that God is in other places too; as J. D. Salinger said, "All we do our whole lives is go from one little piece of Holy Ground to the next."[7] While this place may sensitize me to God's presence, that presence continues everywhere. The lightly mocking voice reviews the itinerary for the next few weeks and laughs: "Did you think I couldn't find San Antonio? Or your office? Or the supermarket?" If God is so fully in this place, the richness spills over. I carry the gazebo within; God goes with me.

Mountains:
Sinai and Tabor in the United States

Pilgrimages to the mountains occur throughout the Hebrew-Christian tradition. The word for mountain appears 520 times in the Old Testament, and one scripture scholar argues that the six mountain stories in Matthew provide the schema which orders that gospel.[8] Like a new Moses, Jesus climbs Mt. Tabor and his transfiguration there becomes the fulfillment of promises made at Mt. Sinai. Always pushing boundaries, Jesus is tempted on a mountain, gathers his community for the sermon on the mount, suffers agony on the Mount of Olives, sends the disciples forth and ascends from the mountain of Galilee "to which Jesus had directed them" (Mt 28:16). Elusive and beautiful, the mountain has always symbolized the human longing for the divine.

How does a twenty-first-century woman, who drives a Toyota to the mountains and stays in a condo there, fit into this tradition? It may seem like a stretch, but if we do not try to configure the lines of our lives to the longer story, we cannot make it our own. We cannot benefit from its broader scope if we have not at least tried to imagine the links between our grandparents in faith and ourselves. Discovering the links is one step toward making a mountain trip sacramental.

While the means of transportation may be different and we no longer regard the mountain as dangerous and remote, some themes remain the same: the mountains are a privileged place for meeting the God of the surprise. The rugged landscape continues to evoke "the deepest desire of the human heart for untamed mystery and beauty."[9] "We want to see the ordinariness of our lives transformed into glory, lifted up to clear view on the horizon of our world, like a snow-capped mountain shimmering in the morning sun."[10]

Such lofty goals are inspired by a phone call from a friend, the generous offer of a night at their condominium in Breckenridge, a ready acceptance. Not knowing what to anticipate, the family arrives and we're delighted: a charming Victorian home, with a hot tub on the porch and a huge cathedral window framing nearby ski slopes. The sun sets pinkly, cozily over the Ten-Mile Range, and a full moon rises.

Then, from the hot tub on the porch, I see a stunning image. Earlier that week, a wise priest had explained how often the race we get caught up in isn't the reality; it's the illusion. The reality is the sustaining love of God, which surely brought me to this place in a long line of pilgrims, and breathes within me, right here, right now. This radiant, unchanging love underlies everything that is, but it takes a nudge like this to see it.

Before me is the perfect symbol of this truth: the moon illuminates a mountain range floating whitely above the village. It drifts in beauty like a cloud, yet it is solid granite, iron-core real. Truly, this world can be a temple or a tomb. Tonight, a moonlit mountainscape speaks of a compassionate Creator poised behind this earthly door. For me as for ancient peoples of many cultures, God reveals God's self in the mountains.

The next morning, the mountains stand tall in the clear, sharp air. I have been graced before to have had such mornings, but never have I sat before such a majestic view, framed as if for me personally. I want to preserve this moment, warm with hazelnut coffee, as I watch the skiers making graceful turns, joyous in this new glimpse of divine reality. What kind of God gives us vast stretches for our delight, high peaks on which to play?

What I discover experientially in the condo, I read later in a book: Wayne Muller's *Sabbath*. He explains that people who find wholeness, strength, and beauty underlying creation "delight in the gift and blessing of being alive." Those who find creation flawed avoid contact with it and work hard "to get the hell out of here." Only the future is good and perfect; today is always a bad day; the promised land alone contains peace and happiness.[11]

The latter is a dismal view of reality but helps explain the grim looks and set jaws of the hell-bent-for-success-overachievers. We all know at least one, who makes us feel guilty for soaking in a hot tub or gazing out the cathedral window. We *could* have been scrubbing the porch, they harrumph—or at least catching up on paperwork from the office, thoughtfully tucked into the briefcase.

I'd rather toy with Muller's rhetorical questions. What if "the promised land we seek is already present in the very gift of life itself, the inestimable privilege of a human birth? What if this single human life is itself the jewel in the lotus, the treasure hidden in the field, the pearl of great price?"[12]

To his musings I add my own: What if a mottled white cloud drifting over mountains is actually a solid symbol of the Holy One's abiding protection and care? For centuries, climbing a mountain has symbolized the human path toward absolute reality. So much beauty along the way energizes; both the destination and the journey are sacraments of the world.

The Great Smokies

A trip to North Carolina during the peak of fall color helps me understand a further refinement of the mountain metaphor for God. Mt. Sinai represents God's awesome, inaccessible, powerful transcendence. Mt. Tabor, on the other hand, is lower, covered in green, the site of the transfiguration, where "in seeing Jesus, [the disciples] also saw themselves anew."[13] Throughout the history of Christianity, "Sinai and

Tabor are identified as complementary dimensions of a single truth."[14]

But theology is not foremost on my mind as, fortified with fresh apples from a roadside stand, I drive the Blue Ridge Parkway. There I discover that a bluish haze does drift over these low mountains, lending them an aura of mystery.

They are solid, gentle hills compared to the raw, jagged Rockies that tower over Breckenridge. Our peaks rip the skies; theirs sleep in mounds like blanketed children. Our waterfalls leap precipitously, spiraling and tossing thousands of feet down sheer crevices, thundering into foam below. Their waterfalls spill sweetly onto mossy rock ledges, barely denting the pool's surface a few feet beneath.

The leaves are spectacular, dramatically different from our golden aspen. In summer I guess they blend into one green tapestry, but now each branch, each leaf is carved unique in eye-popping color. Even the brashest decorator might hesitate to put orange and burgundy smack up against each other; here they flame together. With Zen serenity, the red maple leaf floats to earth, and I think I would not so easily let go of summer.

What is the same here and at home is the vastness, the sense of a national park being endless, a land without boundary. I cross and re-cross state lines blithely because they don't seem to matter here. A day in such a place is a deep wellspring, a glimpse of God who is not remote and distant but intimate and close.

That evening in the hotel, I read the King James translation of the Gideon Bible: "Philip saith unto him, Lord, show us the Father, and it sufficeth us" (Jn 14:8). Aside from the charming Elizabethan courtliness of the Galilean fisherman, I'm struck by one phrase: "it sufficeth us." Could this be key to happiness, this glad recognition of autumn color as coming from God's generous hands?

Mary Oliver describes the day's balance of active sightseeing and grateful reflection:

so this is how you swim inward,
so this is how you flow outward,
so this is how you pray.[15]

Dressing Room

A recent shopping trip designed as an escape-from-writing-the-book brought me right back to everyday sacraments in unexpected places.

As I tried on clothes, I heard a chorus of young voices from the dressing room beside mine. "That's perfect, Mom! You can wear it to the wedding. . . . That is so cute on you—really flattering! . . . You look darling in that one—Mom, you've got to get it!" The sound of voices warm with approval slid over the partitions, and self-esteem gurus would have grinned. From the enthusiastic tone of the cheerleaders, I assumed that she who modeled the fashions was a sleek size 2, a glamorous Nancy Reagan. When I emerged to hunt for larger clothes sizes myself, I got my first surprising glimpse of Mom.

The best description comes from Ilene Beckerman's comparisons of herself to fashion models. They look like bread sticks; her figure is "more akin to a Kaiser roll." They are built like ironing boards; she is "shaped more like an upholstered chair."[16] This mom bore the weight of countless birthday cakes, picnics, and potlucks. Her face was creased by sleepless nights, her posture sloped; her hair needed a trim which had probably been postponed when some child needed a dentist appointment more urgently.

But she was a lucky woman. Surely her young daughters had been relentlessly bombarded by media images of thin = beautiful. They had grown up as we all have in a culture that puts a high priority on appearances. Yet somehow they could set that aside to take on the role of mom's fashion consultants. They knew more important things about her inner fortitude or resourcefulness that had borne them through infancy and croup and toddler-hood and flu and last-minute projects for the art fair.

Although shopping alone that day meant a welcome break for my wallet, the drifting compliments made me miss my own daughters. They have often provided me the dressing room version of the Hallelujah Chorus. We've simulated numerous public speaking occasions and they've offered the honest thumbs up or thumbs down that no sales clerk with a vested interest in my purchase can provide. When their comments are restrained and polite, I know to veer away from some flowery natural inclinations, toward clean lines and flattering colors. They've steered me away from some impulsive bargains that would've been disasters, toward some wise investments that I've worn for years.

On better days, I like to think I've given them some helpful tips in the dressing rooms, too, like what does or doesn't constitute professional wear. (No, the ten-inch skirt is not suitable for the office.) Somewhere in their psyches I've planted a scale of what we can and can't afford, as someone did in mine. They've learned how to phrase criticisms diplomatically—or suffer a retaliatory cut in their clothing budgets. Best of all, they've learned when to quit—when we're getting carried beyond need, or gotten too tired, or spent more on clothing than we can justify in a hungry world.

What makes an interlude in the dressing room a "small s" sacrament? It seems far removed from what we often associate with the sacred: the hushed church, the practiced choir, the dignified leaders in vestments. In a sense, it represents what some preachers caution fervently to avoid: materialism, superficiality, an emphasis on appearance at the cost of a deeper look at human beings.

Yet I believe stubbornly that a certain grace permeates the dressing room where age and beauty cease to matter, honesty reigns, and affirmations abound.

Mothers and daughters reflect each other in a ritual that must stretch back to the days when they admired their stylish new goat skins in the mirror of a stream. Shakespeare captured the relationship in Sonnet 24:

> *Thou art thy mother's glass and she in thee*
> *Calls back the lovely April of her prime. . . .*

In a sense, we're trying on different selves—and those closest to us help us choose the faces that fit.

While the ladies' dressing room has no altar, that's never stopped grace before. It creeps into the unlikeliest cracks and the most unseemly surprises. To appreciate that hide-and-seek play we need a vision based on "the possibility that grace might attend, even unexpectedly burst in upon, the least of our doings."[17]

If that possibility is always there, it helps alleviate the burden of dragging ourselves to the dressing room—or anywhere else—as yet another drudgery. We begin to see how "sacramental rites wait to be replicated in our quotidian lives: simple grace. Unlofty eucharists."[18] The Mormon Tabernacle Choir jammin' in the clothing store.

The Botanic Gardens:
Human Flowering

To winter-starved eyes, yearning for color, June feeds the senses with fragrance, flower, variety. What Hopkins called "all this joy and all this juice" reaches a pitch in the Botanic Gardens, where professional staff and volunteers cultivate twenty-three acres of beauty in the city.

And it's not all flowery-bowery. The story gardens walk children through a magical place called "Where the Wild Things Are"; the Monet gardens re-create the artist's images of watery violet and blue larkspur; the vegetable gardens enable apartment dwellers to work plots of land here. In summer different musical groups perform; today the Cantabile Singers are featured.

They have wisely chosen their program to fit the setting. Across a pink fountain of roses drifts the Song of Songs:

Arise, my love, my fair one
and come away;
for now the winter is past,
the rain is over and gone.
The flowers appear on the earth;
the time of singing has come. . . . (2:10-12)

Centuries before, someone voiced the experience we are having today. Later voices added praise in the same tone. The music of Robert Burns, "For my love is like a red, red rose," sounds beside a crimson patch of the real thing.

On tags carefully identifying each species, the scholarly botanists turn into poets, naming flowers sunburst and starshine, fairy petticoat and honey gold. Their exuberance echoes Adam's naming spree in the first garden. The people strolling the paths echo that delight, pointing out this purple globe or that fuschia cascade as proudly as if they'd planted it.

Down colonnades fit for a queen, the commoners walk with dignity. Overhead hang baskets of trailing lobelia; pastel cushions of peony bloom at either side. The variety of plants feeds the soul: spikes and plumes, velvety leaves and delicate carvings, bending grasses and cottony clouds. The colors chorus: apricot, burgundy, lavender, and hot pink are tangled together. To be steeped in so much beauty tranquilizes; to be surrounded by so much life energizes.

From the vantage point of an office later in the week, the gardens become even more of a haven. Disputes drain energy; tension clouds work; trivia consumes too much time. The combined music of madrigal and fountain drifts too far away. No scents grace the stuffy air.

But I believe, if God lurks in the garden, God lurks everywhere. At other times, God *has* been clearly present in the office. But it is June, the air is soft, and maybe even God would rather go to the garden. There God once walked with Adam. There Jesus took on the role of the gardener who intervened to protect a fig tree that did not flower. There he startled Mary Magdalene who mistook him for the gardener.

Garden Transformed

In John's account, Mary Magdalene stands in the place of grieving, lonely, confused humanity. Her struggle is the same one we all face—in the midst of politics, brutality, a confused community, grieving, and desolation—to find the absent Jesus. And like many of us, she looks in all the wrong places. The Song of Songs that had drifted across the Botanic Gardens is the theme of her quest:

I sought him whom my soul loves;
I sought him, but found him not;
I called him, but he gave no answer.
"I will rise now and go about the city,
in the streets and in the squares;
I will seek him whom my soul loves."
I sought him, but found him not. (3:1-2)

We sometimes say we're stuck between a rock and a hard spot—but Mary's stuck between a boulder and a corpse. And she doesn't know how the story ends. Mary experiences utter devastation—not only does her best friend die a brutal death, but now the corpse has been taken away. That means she's lost the one thing she knows from her tradition to do: anoint the precious body.

In the face of the most cataclysmic event in human history, she's sleepless, confused, fretful. No one would blame her—throughout the history of humankind, dead people have stayed dead. No corpse has moved itself. It's the most natural thing in the world for her to assume an outside agent, and the gardener is the likely candidate.

That's why Jesus' calling her name is so important: it's the turning point of the whole story, *and* of human history. If Jesus could come back from death, he could beat any obstacle, overcome any impediment to being with those he loves. In his calling of her name must be all tenderness but at the same time, all power, the power that brushes death aside like a gnat on the ankle.

"Now I come to you," he says, "and my power is in you. You pivot from being the anointer to being the announcer." It turns out Jesus has been with Mary all along, just as he is with us when we never suspected. He says, "You don't need to cling to me so tight, honey.

I'll always be around. From now on, I live in your heart—and not only yours, but everyone's." So we could all conclude with the Songs of Songs:

> *when I found him whom my soul loves,*
> *I held him and would not let him go. (3:4)*

The action has shifted from tomb to garden, and the garden flourishes within. All that is desolate in us will someday flower.

Home

Unlock the door. Check the mail. Replace dressy clothes with sweatshirt and jeans. Make huge mug of coffee laced with French vanilla cream. Light scented candle. Ease into armchair. Elevate feet. Snuggle into flannel wrap. Rest contorted neck. Sigh loudly. Sink into Eliza Doolittle's dream come true: "warm face, warm hands, warm feet: now wouldn't it be loverly?"

The realists protest: "What about feed the dog? start dinner? calm screaming children competing greedily for attention? check calendar of evening activities?" Granted, all those are part of the homecoming ritual too. But here we focus on the ideal scenario, the most life-giving, relaxing routine—that we all wish we had! While all of it may be impossible, at least one component might be doable. Or perhaps it might be doable after all the other business is handled.

Assuming that myriad details are attended to—and this may well be 10 p.m.—ease into prayer. Begin to recapture identity as daughter or son of God, a role camouflaged by eight hours as workhorse. Read a scripture passage like this:

> *"In my Father's house there are many dwelling places. If it were not so, would I have told you that I go to prepare a place for you? And if I go and prepare a place for you, I will come again and will take you to myself, so that where I am, there you may be also." (Jn 14:2-3)*

A friend tells me that Jesus' imagery comes from the marriage custom of his day. When a father decided his son was ready for marriage, he brought him to the public square, where the son would make an indentation of his sandal in the dust. This was the signal to the young women, whose parents would bring them to the marketplace. When one woman placed her sandalprint within the print of the man's, it signaled the time for a betrothal.

The family would then bargain over the dowry and conclude their negotiations with a feast of bread and wine. One step remained: the man returned to his hovel and began adding a room for his bride. He made this promise as he told her farewell: "In my father's house, there are many dwelling places. . . . I go and prepare a place for you so that where I am, there you may be also."

We do not have to wait for heaven to enter this place. As Beatrice Bruteau points out, we can read Jesus' words to the good thief not as a promise but as a plea to us now: "Be with me in paradise."[19] So maybe the whole day won't be paradisical. But these few moments can be, at twilight in the armchair, with the neck relaxed, the feet propped, and the stresses soothed.

We have all known the pleasure of a dreadful place shared with someone we love. The hike in the rain, the boring movie, the road trip from hell, the lousy restaurant, or the roach motel all lose their horrors when we have someone to share the experience and laugh uproariously—or surreptitiously, if the inept waiter is hovering. From the human way of sharing experience, it's not a huge leap to the divine way: "so that where I am, you may be also."

Few people are conscious of being in God's presence all the time. Outside influences blur that bottom-line reality and we forget the One who goes with us always and everywhere. Yet we shouldn't feel guilty—the people who surrounded Jesus during his time on earth were rarely attuned to his identity, and Peter for one made some spectacular faux-pas about Jesus.

What does it take to awaken us? Sometimes just the relief of a secure place and a rest after work. It doesn't take an ocean or a mountain, though those often do the job quite nicely. An armchair works . . . a candle . . . a cup of coffee . . . a blanket. The place is prepared. In this unspectacular sanctuary, I am with God. What could matter more?

Aquarium:
Another Sunday Reverence

It's Sunday morning and I'm not the only one entering a watery temple instead of a church. What draws so many people here? Part of the attraction is sheer beauty: pulsing parachutes of jellyfish look like lacy parasols of light. Their easy undulation could be set to Debussy and we could name them a swimming star, a floating petal of moonlight. Some fish wear a Joseph's coat of butterfly wings; their fluttering soothes the psyche.

Another draw is the chance to view creation in its staggering variety—intricacies and playfulness, color and adaptation. We see a wide range—from fish that look like flowers to tiny dart frogs that look like they're painted with jade Chinese lacquer. On this first day of the week, the aquarium celebrates Genesis: "Let the waters bring forth swarms of living creatures."

The aquarium gives entry to a larger world where we are citizens, however remotely. Even those who have not strolled beside the sea glistening with needles of light or a bay gone soft with silver have the chance to open a little window on Oceanus here.

So it invites intense interest across generations, ethnicities, and economic levels. The three-year-old Japanese girl, delicate as a doll, stands beside the hulking, tattooed biker with the ponytail. She and he are equally absorbed in the sight of sleek shark or the wild neon coloring of tropical fish. The awe and wonder of these visitors—not only the children—would be the envy of liturgists who encourage "full, conscious, and active participation."

For the pragmatic, the sign informs that these creatures the size of a little fingernail may contain some key to the treatment of cancer. Even the gray sheaf of shark may help find the cure for AIDS. In a typically Christian paradox, the misnamed killer may cruise the sea with healing clues. Squinting into cavernous tanks, we wonder what other mysteries the seas might unveil.

Most people probably enjoy aquariums at that level, which is indeed rich enough. But for the Christian, all this water bubbles with symbolic overtones.

We would see not just the water in fonts and the bread and wine on altars as communicating the presence of God in Christ. All waters, meals, forests and fields, flora and fauna; all creeping, crawling, swimming, slithering, prancing, dancing creatures and all those that hum and chirp and go bump in the night . . . air, fire and water throughout all creation—all these become sacraments of God's presence.[20]

St. Ambrose of Milan, a fourth-century father of the church, reminded his listeners that the waters of Genesis teemed with life, and recent visitors to aquariums can attest to the fact. Drenched in this variety, we are sensitized to his analogy: just as creatures were brought forth from the sea, so the baptized are born through the waters.

"So even for you this world is a sea. It has diverse floods, heavy waters, severe storms. And do you be a fish, that the water of the world may not submerge you."[21] It's not simply an exercise in fantasy when we ask children gazing into a tank, "What kind of fish would you be?" Aquariums remind us that at some level, we are all amphibian. To move easily between land and sea, reverencing their marvels, is indeed a grace, a "small s" sacrament.

Rita's Field

My friend tells me the story of her sacred place and I find myself turning it over and over in my mind, like a jewel in the hand. Although I've never been to her place, I know it somehow; it resonates so closely with some of my own. What common thread sanctifies such places? Why are we drawn to them as to fire on a cold night?

Let's hold the questions while we visit Rita's field, forty acres behind her parents' home in Iowa. A creek runs through it and prairie wildflowers bloom there abundantly. As a child, she would ride her pony there after school, her way of calming herself and dealing with the day's events. But she never realized how important it was to her until after college graduation.

Returning home after the painful end of a relationship she thought would lead to marriage, she moped around the house for three days. Her mother listened patiently to the whining, but on the third day said, "Enough. Get on your horse and ride through that field. Then get off and dig in the earth, even if it's frozen. Get yourself grounded again."

Rita took the advice, worked through the crisis, and several years later, took another young man named Bob to see the field. It turned out Bob's grandparents had first homesteaded that area. Her relationship with him grew serious, and the day before her birthday, he asked her to walk through the field with him. From the hillside, Rita could see her grandmother's farm, her aunt and uncle's acreage, and land belonging to Bob's family.

"Our ancestors farmed these fields and made a productive life here," Bob said. "I'd like to do that with you." He offered her an engagement ring, and the field took on a new significance. To Bob and Rita's children it would always be the place they got engaged. Even though the family moved to the city, they visited the farm often. After Rita's mom died, she remembers driving the children through the field on a four-wheeler at sunset, watching deer emerge from the willows and the moon rising. Later that week in school, asked to describe her sacred place, her daughter told the story of the field.

To introduce the concept of sacred place to her students, Rita showed them a picture of her daughter running through the field, wildflowers up to her knees. Although Bob and Rita eventually sold the field to her nephew, they kept it in the family. He has built a "deer watch" station there, where he takes his daughter to observe the animals.

I have never been to Iowa, but I like to hang around Rita's field, imagining the scents and textures of the grasses, the rippling of the brook. I like to think of it greening in spring, or silent under winter snow. M. F. K. Fisher once described such a place: it invites you to come well before your departure, and to linger on after your arrival.[22] Its details and colorations are etched on the soul.

Furthermore, it is the setting for story; life's intricate nuances, happinesses, and disappointments are played out on that stage. Carol Flinders comments, "In a *place*, something hangs in the air—a life, a spirit. You are held there not merely by comfort, but by interest and expectation: important things go on here. . . ."[23] For years, Carol's favorite way to drift off to sleep has been to mentally reconstruct her grandparents' farm in the Willamette Valley. Having recalled the primroses, Concord grapes, chickens, wood stove, and quilts, she becomes "swathed . . . in such unutterable security that nothing on earth could keep me awake."[24]

I suspect that a place like Rita's field or Carol's farm grounds the healthiest psyches: a particular stretch of beach, a favorite B & B, a certain city block, a hillside in sunlight, a forest. Whether we are there in actuality or in memory, it connects us to a deep source, a hidden treasure, an underground river of happiness. We can spend a long time teasing out its warm echoes, its implications for life.

We who love place delight in the fact that God chose to become incarnate in a village named Bethlehem, grew up in a town called Nazareth, taught in the marketplace of Galilee and sailed its sea, prayed in a garden, suffered on a hill named Calvary, and rose from a tomb near Jerusalem. In doing so, Jesus blessed all our sacred places and shared our affection for the earth, the sea, the skies.

What kind of culture produces this wild out-pouring of art, this crazy explosion of color? Nowhere else would a decorator attempt such uncoordinated color schemes; here, they work. Purple sidles up to ruby, coral and bright blue are partners, peach and crimson get along. A lust for beauty blossoms everywhere we turn—even the bathroom tiles flower. To some extent, it is the result of blending Native American, Spanish, and French influences, but other places have this mix too—without the flourishing art. To some extent it is due to climate and terrain, but other spots have clear skies and high mountains too—still without the art.

Having no scientific explanation, I wonder if it can be traced to some influence of the Catholic sacramental imagination. Anchoring the old cities of Santa Fe, Taos, and Albuquerque are mission churches, which Andrew Greeley calls "strongholds of the analogical imagination, . . . treasure houses of stories of God's presence in the human condition."[25] Hence, they ground and inspire "great works of art shaped by religious imagination,"[26] even if artists aren't consciously aware of their influence.

The image of Mary permeates the area—not only directly, in statues of Guadalupe and crèches, but subtly, in the warm, feminine curve of adobe. Its rounded clay shapes frame a turquoise sky above, and could well shelter an infant below.

"In the art and the music and the poetry of Catholics, Mary's image clearly reflects the tenderness of God," and hence has enormous appeal.[27] The history of the Southwest is a brutal saga of murder, greed, violence, and oppression. Yet despite the mayhem, one finds at its core the madonna image, "irresistible to human nature since it represents the ongoing triumph of fertility over morbidity, of life over death."[28] Such persistent hope gives impetus to art.

This is not a culture that reflects the depression of a dreary world in dark, gray interiors or stark, undecorated walls. Instead, this art depicts burning azure skies and pink mountains bristling with piñon pine. Interior decoration exalts every native hummingbird and cactus flower. Frescoes and designs drawn from nature fill every space. Hot blasts of geraniums and cobalt clouds of lobelia spill over every patio.

Browsing through art galleries, a bold stroke of scarlet or a buttery pool on canvas captures what we have all known at some time. That fiery blotch or that delicate field recalls mornings when all was soaring and bright. The day filled with such potential that the mere act of arising was a privileged threshold to surprise. Mary Oliver describes these times and their effect: "What is one to do with such moments, such memories, but cherish them?" Afterward, "would you not live in continual hope and pleasure and excitement?"[29]

In the sculpture gardens, a statue captures the careful stance of a little boy with a watering can. A little girl with a book is caught in bronze, as if preserved in amber, so that one looks anew at one's own little girl. The sculpted line of children playing crack-the-whip captures the tossed shoe, the swished skirt, the heavy hair, and we realize again how charming human children can be.

Art brings us back to real life, and in Santa Fe the lines between natural and artful beauty are blurred. One strolls from painted gardens into the real thing; the observer studies molded adobe in the framed canvas, then observes it in the gallery's roof. After a day at museums, we return to a hotel with a resident artist and sleep beneath hand-painted headboards. In Taos one out of ten residents makes a living from art.

What does art's beautiful calligraphy tell us of sacrament? Both return us with more earnest intent to the lived experience. The doors of the museum, like the doors of the church, lead inexorably back to the world. The artist, like the contemplative, teaches us to take "a long, loving look at the real."

The medium for Georgia O'Keeffe was image, not religious language. But what prompted her painting was a close and reverent observation of nature: "Every morning a little drop of dew would have run down the veins [of corn] into the center of this plant like a little lake—all fine and fresh."[30] "I . . . sat on the fence for a long time—just looking at the lightning." O'Keeffe's friend "Ted Reid remembered her rapt attentiveness to dramatic weather: 'Did you ever see her watch a great storm? There was never anyone in the world like her in her appreciation of such things.'"[31]

Except possibly Thomas Merton, whose father was an artist. Even before he knew anything about God, Merton inherited a sacramental view of reality. While his father didn't consider himself a "religious" man, his respect for creation spoke in his paintings. Later, the Trappist monk became absorbed in photography as a way to express God's presence in all things. His photos of tree trunk or watering can, barn or basket draw attention to textures or shapes we might otherwise miss.

As a boy, Merton lived with his father in the medieval city of St. Antonin, France. The pattern of the village focused on the church; its steeple dominated the town. As in New Mexico, the church's centrality announced the purpose of creation. Merton's comment on St. Antonin could apply to Santa Fe or Taos: "What a thing it is, to live in a place that is so constructed that you are forced, in spite of yourself, to be at least a virtual contemplative!"[32] Never underestimate the power of such a place.

Fishin' Hole:
The Retrieval of Memory

As everything else in the family's life undergoes transition, we like to visit a tiny wooden cabin in a remote corner of Colorado where nothing seems to change. We have been coming here for twenty years, and the routine is always familiar and sweet. Every year on the drive there, we see more new building, but the sign at the general store continues to proclaim in happy hokiness, "A friendly hello and a good buy." Some things in the universe should remain forever.

The wild exotic call of the cranes still drifts across vast spaces, and the lungs pull deep breaths of this air scented with sage. In the city our breathing is shallow; here it is deep as must have been intended at creation. Clouds shadow the mountains; wind wrinkles the blue bowl of the lake; deer roam freely. Every pencil-slim aspen trunk is reflected in the water's crystalline mirror. At evening, brushed by silver, the lake clings to the last vestiges of light. A zebra-striped butterfly seems magnetized to a deep blue flower.

When the children were small it was paradise for them; the catching of crawdads and the rowing of boats and the forays into glacial waters filled their days. Now their tastes have graduated to renting a pontoon on the larger lake nearby. There, the snowy peaks are distant ramparts and the waters sparkle. Everyone grins with pure delight as the kids sun on the boat deck. Life is expansive; time is luxurious; for two hours we have no worries other than piloting the pontoon.

Having recently returned from New Mexico, I compare the landscape. There, the round frame for our little life-stage was adobe and carnelian-colored hills.

Here, blue-green hills encircle us like a shawl that could be pulled around the shoulders for warmth. There, we calibrated the heat of different chiles. Here, we eat freshly caught rainbow trout for dinner, praising the fisherfolk who snagged them the night before.

"Memory is the simplest form of prayer" writes Marge Piercy in her poem "Black Mountain." If that is true, then parents of young adults must spend a lot of time praying. The place kindles the memory; after the older children bustle back to their jobs, I meet again the four little ghosts of their childhoods.

Once we photographed the "baby" lying on the lawn beside recently caught trout that all outweighed her. Now she is fifteen, much in demand as a babysitter. *In a secluded cove, a two-year-old bangs his shovel on his sand pail. His sturdy legs are like anchors; wisps of strawberry blonde hair peek out like spills of sun beneath his red cowboy hat.* He's a college sophomore now; his internship beckons louder than the sand pail.

Across the lake a young girl and boy pilot a canoe; she is eight and he is ten. They are careful and concerted in their effort because taking the boat out alone is a rare privilege they won't risk losing. How many projects they've collaborated on since then with the same intense concentration! Now they burrow into plans for graduate school and international travel. We buy the family cell phone plan so they can keep in touch across long distances.

For years, I read to toddlers here, who later brought stacks of their own books and called "dibs" on the reading chair beneath the only decent light. The evenings are long and uninterrupted by the telephone, television, or computers that consume our time at home. We've begun and ended many a fine novel here, and I think with pleasure of a fundraiser my older son recently chaired. Did the $100,000 he raised for the Children's Literacy Center have its dim beginnings in a boy bent over books in a tiny mountain cabin?

Rumors about a stranger from New York leasing the cabin for all of next summer threaten our annual vacation. We are at once disturbed and more appreciative of the recurring blessing this place has been. How rare it must be for a family to return to the same oasis of beauty for twenty years, drawing from it warmth, connection, and healing.

Mary Pipher, an expert in family life, staunchly proclaims the value of special places to protect families. She admits to a bias for natural settings such as lakeside or mountain cabins, and concludes that in a family's sacred place it's impossible to not feel sheltered, "safe, temporarily at ease in our difficult universe."[33]

Even if we could not return to our fishin' hole, an imaginary banner will always stretch over the cabin door, proclaiming, "We were happy here." A place where we can enjoy each other and recall our history must be holy ground. It is lodged forever in memory, etched in the heart's deep recesses, and cannot be taken away.

The Ramada Inn Retreat

I knew I'd been traveling too much when I made the Ramada Inn Retreat. It happened like this. . . .

Flying into Louisville, Kentucky, I was elated. For twenty years, I had read Thomas Merton, chortled at his irreverence, seized on his insights, and reveled in his poetry. When an opportunity arose to visit his hometown, I bought his newest journal and made plans to stay with his old friend and my mentor, Sister Mary Luke Tobin. (I've written about *her* before, a woman who deserves a whole book about her contributions to Vatican Council II, the peace movement, and the rights of women.)

After a workshop in Louisville, I'd drive to Nerinx, where Sister Luke now lived. At last I'd see the blue hills shading the abbey at Gethsemani, which Merton described so poetically. With any luck I'd visit the corner of 4th and Walnut (now Muhammad Ali) where he had his profound insight that people were walking around shining like the stars. I wanted a geography known only from books to take on the shape and texture of reality. Anyone who has searched for Samuel Johnson's London, Shakespeare's Stratford-on-Avon, or Monet's garden recognizes the instinct.

But plans made in June had not included the snows of January. Stranded by a blizzard, I couldn't see Sister Luke, Nerinx, or Gethsemani, and was stuck in a nondescript airport motel with a long stretch of time 'til the next flight home. The view out the window was bleak; snow iced the asphalt parking lot and the adjoining Whiz Mix factory. Speculation about *that* product was mildly amusing, but ultimately unfulfilling. So I turned to the savvy traveler's store of books, or in this case, Thomas Merton's Journal, Volume Six.

The subtitle abounds in irony. *Learning to Love* is not a spiritual cliché, but must also refer to the author's affair with a student nurse. While I knew that part of Merton lore, I'd heard it dismissed lightly by his fans. They joked nervously about Tom in his early fifties falling head-over-heals for M., the only way she is ever named. Perhaps out of consideration for her, Merton specified that the journals not be published until twenty-five years after his death.

But the more I read, the deeper I plunged into his anguish. What had been glossed over by most biographers was in fact a crisis that plummeted Merton into the terrible aloneness of Christ. For the first time in his life, he knew what it meant to be cherished just as he was by a woman who was "achingly sweet," open, and tender. She was simple and spontaneous; he realized "that the deepest capacities for human love in me have never even been tapped, that I too can love with an awful completeness. Responding to her has opened up the depths of my life in ways I can't begin to understand or analyze now."[34]

One has to admire Merton for taking a risk that he knew would lead to serious danger. In fact, when his "affair" was discovered, the abbot imposed harsh penalties: an abrupt end, with no possibility of contact between them ever again.

Yet Merton insisted that love was not a problem, simply an impossibility. Despite the leering, "boy scout" gallery of "good" monks, he remained convinced that loving M. did not mean infidelity to his vocation. Instead, his love for her was part of his love for Christ. "If God has brought her into my life and if God has willed our love, then it is more [God's] affair than ours."[35]

His words sound prophetic in a world where a priest loving a woman was anathema. For such a "calamity," the institution would call out all its hounds. Sounding remarkably like a citizen of the twenty-first century, Merton refuses to swallow the official line: "There comes a time when all this legal machinery for fulmination simply does not convince. It claims to be the voice of God, it pretends to damn in His name and by His authority. . . . Does it really?"[36]

While I admired Merton's courage and honesty, the jail-sentence to the Ramada Inn would teach me less about Merton than about God. Merton's willingness to speak out with an open heart, to pay his "debt to life," becomes a scaffolding on which to build a personal testimony. The clearly articulated experience of any strong writer enables the reader to empathize, to see the connections with one's own experience, and to approach closer the complex mystery of God.

From Merton's anguish, so like that of any sensitive human being, he learns that God is "as small as myself and as present as myself and we are both nothing and both lonely. That both God and I are lost. And that this is the beginning of everything."[37] What a marvelous turn from triumphalism to a God we have almost forgotten: small at Bethlehem, vulnerable at Bethany, torn apart with pain on Calvary. In our glorious celebrations, robust hymns, and clear convictions, we seldom remember the God who was always aligned with the little ones, the exiles, the small, confused remnant— never the powerful or pure.

The implications are humbling. If I am lost somewhere between the airport and the Whiz Mix Corporation, so is God. If clear-cut pronouncements make me long for honest, gray uncertainty, maybe God shares the doubt. In the face of all this absurdity, God is small and lonely too.

It is a dimension of God too little emphasized, perhaps because it doesn't appeal to the influential and the powerful. Indeed, God *is* beyond all our imaginings, larger than this world, greater than any idea we can frame. Few people want a God small enough to lasso with limited minds. Face it: we need the oomph of God's power, the trumpet call of St. Patrick summoning the Trinity, to get us out of bed in the morning. So the balance lies in complementarity—or, in traditional words, God is both immanent and transcendent. It is the kind of paradox poets play with: all-powerful hands pinned by nails to a cross, the Creator of the universe within the womb of a young girl.

On a dismal morning in an unlikely place, Merton and M. give me a whole new concept of faith: as hanging-around-in-case, befriending the absurd, showing up, resisting the easy answer, refusing to believe that God is "the kind of joker that would want us to believe that the senseless makes sense."[38] Confronting the abyss becomes easier when a presence might be lurking there. That's what incarnation is all about, isn't it? That God is one like me and shares a lonely lot, however bizarre it may be. I pack my suitcase and smile a little, thinking how a stark stretch can flower, a white desert can color.

The Monterey Peninsula

O f the many places that nurture the soul, the Monterey Peninsula is one of the most beautiful. Its green-gold hills and profusion of flowers dazzle the eyes of the winter-weary. Flying in from a barren landscape, we feel like we have returned to Eden. Spring there comes long before spring in the Rocky Mountains; with a devilish delight, we jump-start the process.

John Steinbeck is an articulate voice for this region which he lovingly describes in *Cannery Row*. "Cannery Row in Monterey in California is a poem, a stink, a grating noise, a quality of light, a tone, a habit, a nostalgia, a dream." We who no longer see its bustling sardine fleet, honky-tonks, and flophouses can still appreciate its broad bays and gracious vistas, seagulls and sunsets.

Living in such friendly surroundings must have enhanced Steinbeck's reverence for his characters.

> *Its inhabitants are, as the man once said, "whores, pimps, gamblers, and sons of bitches," by which he meant Everybody. Had the man looked through another peephole he might have said, "saints and angels and martyrs and holy men," and he would have meant the same thing.*[39]

This "double vision" of people is distinctly Christian, seeing in the same glance the warts and the beloved child of God. Visitors strolling the wharf half expect to encounter the friendly ghosts of Doc Ricketts the marine biologist, Mack and the boys, Dora the madame, and Lee Chong the grocer.

Even if the cast is less colorful now, some things about the region remain distinctive: the menus of fresh seafood, the smell of seaweed, the bark of sea lions, the echo of waves, the cascading wisteria, the pearly light of early morning. As the soul settles into such a landscape, it finds the refreshment of a deep breath or a long nap. Any trouble that might impinge here would be handled by a separate lobe of the brain, separate from such content.

Further south on the coast lies Carmel, a village from an English fairy tale. We stay there in a bed and breakfast overlooking the sea. The afternoon ritual is civilized: sherry and Scrabble by the fire. The morning walk is another visit to the soul's home, among misted jade hills swirling down to the beach like silken skirts.

The fragrance of sweet alyssum which covers the hills drifts upward on the ocean breeze. The cove below creates a perfect image for the kind circle of God's embrace. On both sides, the arms of land enclose the harbor. So the beauty of water is cupped by the curved shore, but open sea beckons beyond—an invitation to the infinite.

The place mirrors two poles of human experience: longing and belonging. The safe shores represent our grounding in earth, green and solid. The ocean beckons to the unknown, the mysterious reach without which we'd shrivel into apathy or boredom.

John O'Donohue reminds us that Celtic spirituality gives "a clear view of the sacrament of Nature."[40] What people worship offers a clue to what they understand as the source of life; for the Celts, certain wells, trees, and animals were sacred. They worshiped in wild groves. Today we usually worship indoors; within the church we approach God through word and ritual.

But perhaps we're missing something in the set text and prescribed gesture. In the vast outdoors, we appreciate the God who cannot be contained within boundaries. Joyce Rupp writes of a "lifeless liturgy": "what

truly stirs my soul is beyond the wooden walls."
Coming home from church, she wants to stop the car,
dance in the corn fields,

and fill my flat religion
with joy of another kind.[41]

One benefit of travel is its stimulation to think differently, see afresh, reflect in new ways. Or, in this case,
to become like an ancient Celt overlooking Carmel Bay.
Seeing there the curved image of divine care lifts the
heart; the soul wants to dance a jig in praise.

PART TWO

People: "Kindness to Spare"

The personhood of God, dazzling in variety, comes in filtered ways through the human person. A sacramental view of the person sees Christ coming to life in each one, over and over again. Edward Schillebeeckx said these fresh and radiant possibilities create "new memories of Jesus."

Sometimes we glaze over the faces we see often, or tune out the familiar voice. But when circumstances or deliberate intention lead us to look more carefully, we can see people as direct embodiments of grace, incarnate encounters with God. C. S. Lewis captures this insight as he addresses God:

So it was you all along.
Everyone I ever loved, it was you.
Everything decent or fine that ever happened to me,
everything that made me reach out and try to be better,
it was you all along.

Because the principle of sacramentality underscores God's presence in *all* people, this book focuses on people encountered in the ordinary rounds of an ordinary day: friends, teachers, children, strangers. In "Sailing to Byzantium," Yeats called them "the singing-masters of my soul." There we find the quiet courtesy of Christ, the refusal to let details sap his strength, his joy in creation, his staunch challenge to injustice. Through ordinary faces shines a staggering variety, a breathtaking holiness.

As you read this section, be sensitive to the question:

In what people do you find God?

Then spend some time in reflection or discussion about those you have named.

A Reflection on People:
The Many Faces of Christ

Since when . . .
Are the first line and last line of any poem
Where the poem begins and ends?[1]

—*Seamus Heaney*

L ike the poem to which Heaney refers, the life of Jesus does not begin and end with the first line and last line of the gospels. Not bound now by physical limitations, he continues to live among us in varied and vivid ways.

How do we experience Jesus today? While he still surprises, he probably continues doing through human beings what he did in his earthly life. He thought these actions important enough to weigh in Matthew's account of the final judgment:

> *Then the king will say to those on his right, "You have my Father's blessing; come, take possession of the kingdom that has been ready for you since the world was made. For when I was hungry, you gave me food; when thirsty, you gave me drink; when I was a stranger, you took me into your home; when naked, you clothed me; when I was ill, you came to my help; when in prison, you visited me."(25:34-36, REB)*

We are so accustomed to thinking of these directives as things that we should *do*, that we rarely think of the other side of the coin: how we've been the *recipients*. Most folks would agree it's harder to be on the receiving end, easier to do the feeding, clothing, and welcoming ourselves. But only people who have actually been hungry or thirsty know how reverently to give food and drink. Only those who have been desperately sick or lonely can appreciate the welcome touch or the reassuring sound of a visitor's voice.

We cannot do unto others what we have not first experienced ourselves. If we have no experiential base for these kindnesses, how will we recognize our opportunities to do them? If we are preoccupied with our own pain, it is difficult to reach out to anyone. So it is helpful to reflect on how Christ has come through the people who have done us these kindnesses.

Turn the "you" of the gospel passage around, thinking of "you" as Jesus, not ourselves. After each personal remembrance comes a question. This is how it happened in my own life, but how has it happened in *yours*? That unwritten answer thus becomes the most crucial part of this reflection.

For when I was hungry, you gave me food . . .

Being the cook most of the time makes me especially grateful for others' cooking. Many years ago a friend from college met my flight at the Orange County airport, drove to Laguna Beach, and produced a cooler to celebrate a birthday, including chocolate-dipped strawberries! The mother of five children, she has honed her knack for finding the perfect food to fit the feast. A kind host once made me breakfast, simply because he knew I did it so often for others. I ate my cereal and drank my coffee like royalty that day.

Most memorable meals nourish the spirit as well as the body. At Thanksgiving, Christmas, or birthday banquets, the stories that circulate the table are just as important as the dishes passed around it. We cherish times when "food for the journey" has come on two planes: we left the table strengthened not only by calories, but by conversation.

Beauty, too, can feed the spirit. When we are exhausted or depressed, the sight of a lovely lake, flowering meadow, or towering tree can lift the spirits. Who can deny that Christ gives the burst of energy that ensues, the spark we so desperately need?

When you were hungry, who fed you?

. . . when thirsty, you gave me drink . . .

Sometimes we can thirst for affirmation as much as for water. At times in our lives when we are shaky or insecure, Christ comes in the guise of a compliment, the security of a friendship.

After drafting the first chapters of what would eventually become my book *Hidden Women of the Gospels*, I was filled with hope but uncertain. Could an approach to the New Testament that was so different, so geared to women ever be accepted? With trepidation I showed the manuscript to my spiritual director. I shall always remember his quick response: "It's magnificent." He probably exaggerated, but his words gave the grace to continue. On the strength of such assurance, we can walk a dry and dusty path.

Those who long for family are sometimes rewarded with the gift of children or another relationship. The births of my children answered a long thirst, nine months of anticipation and worry. Each child arriving unique, given in total trust, growing and blossoming—no wonder we celebrate each one with champagne! So too a lonely person sometimes finds an unexpected intimacy. Christ comes through a person who is the answer to prayer, the rain after drought.

When you were thirsty, who gave you a drink?

. . . when I was a stranger, you took me into your home . . .

We owe a great debt to those who sheltered us in childhood. Let's start with our parents, who brought us as infants into their lives, probably not dreaming how much expense, disruption, and worry we would cause.

Let's look too at the wider circle of friends and relatives who in one way or another welcomed us into their homes.

Later in life, we may take a spouse or dear friend into the home of ourselves, becoming for the other the person of Christ. Colleagues welcome us to new work situations; neighbors help us feel at home in a new setting.

The first few times I went to a nearby retreat house, I felt insecure about the routines, uncomfortable in the silences. But every morning as I bumbled to the coffee pot, one outgoing, elderly Jesuit would see me coming. Disregarding the signs about silence, he'd bellow across the dining room, "Sweetheart!" Everyone would grin; I'd hug him, and the day would start well. In unfamiliar surroundings, he put me at ease.

Who welcomed you when you felt like a stranger?

. . . when naked, you clothed me . . .

Clothing has always had spiritual significance, from the wedding garment of Isaiah (61:10) to the white gown of baptism. But it's hard to understand the symbolism in scripture or sacrament unless we have first been clothed on the most natural plane. One of the most powerful scenes in the movie *Romero* occurs after the archbishop has had a brutal encounter with the military regime. He emerges from a violent scene naked to the waist; when his people hang his stole around his neck, they are vesting him with more than cloth. They are restoring the dignity of his priesthood.

Those who criticize consumerism are right to remind us of our obligations to the poor. But sometimes "retail therapy" can boost a sagging spirit or prepare for a special event. I don't know if better-behavior-when-well-dressed is gender-related. But I suspect a new shirt sometimes prompts more graciousness and tolerance than a homily does.

"You go girl!" is a frequent refrain from the dressing room when my daughters and I try on clothes. They encourage me to break stodgy molds, try new colors and styles. From the maternal perspective, I delight in their slender young figures, and with absolutely no bias, think they look beautiful in almost everything.

In some hotel room of the future, I'll be dressing to give a talk. As I pull the suit or the blouse out of my suitcase, I'll return mentally to a dressing room with my daughters. The joy of that shopping spree will spill over as I look in the mirror, and later stand at the podium. The clothing is metaphor for the gifts of respect and confidence we give each other.

Who has clothed you in beauty or honor?

. . . when I was ill, you came to my help . . .

When we are sick, we are vulnerable. We surrender our usual control and land (with some grumpiness) in the care of others. While caring for the sick is surely a work of mercy, *being* sick is a strain on anyone's good humor. Whether it's the severe pain of serious illness or the discombobulation of the flu, it unravels our independence and forces us to rely on the kindness of others.

A tonsillectomy at age twenty-nine is no picnic; at that advanced age, no doctor misleads a patient with the cheery encouragement, "Kids bounce right back!" But chronic infections at twenty-nine made surgery my only recourse. I remember waking in a hospital bed with a killer sore throat, late at night. My husband sat in a metal folding chair beside me, sound asleep, still holding my hand. The face of Christ bends over the sick. . . .

After one of our sons had surgery several days before Christmas, we were warned that he couldn't come into contact with anyone else who was ill. So we were distraught when his brother came down with strep. Yet on Christmas Eve, his pediatrician left his own family and came to the office to administer penicillin. When we thanked him for his generosity, he

demurred, "Can't have a little guy sick—or conta-
gious—on Christmas!" "O Come Emmanuel," we'd
prayed in Advent, never anticipating how "God with
us" would come in healing.

Who helped when you were ill?

. . . when in prison, you visited me.

Jail ministry deserves our utmost respect. Many of
us wonder if we'd ever be able to do it, and we admire
those who regularly bring joy and laughter to the cold
world of the penal institution. To many who would
never receive it, they bring outside stimulation, the
warmth of forgiveness, the promise of transformation.
But what of those on the *inside*?

Women inmates speak of their friendships, Christ's
care wearing khaki uniforms. If they are to survive,
they must rely on each other to buoy their hopes, drag
them to support groups, insist that they take every
opportunity for education or training. Deprived of
everything that motivates people outside the walls,
they learn gratitude for the smallest sacramentals: a
view of the sky beyond bars, a rabbit who visits their
garden. They view themselves with brutal honesty:
"I'm an alcoholic and a murderer." Because they are
without pretensions, their integrity would stun the
world outside.

If we have never been incarcerated, we need to
think more broadly about this one. But even those without prison records know the misery of being caged in
depression, pessimism, addiction, or self-doubt.
Alcoholics Anonymous has been for many people the
key in the lock; the fidelity of an AA sponsor who inter-
venes during a 3 a.m. crisis exemplifies the "wounded
healer."

Sometimes when caught up in anxiety or stress, I
have been rescued by friends. The laughing voice that
invites me to lunch, the jokes that keep me grounded,
the casual comment, or the serious conversation—all

can restore perspective. When we are sunk in despair, it's almost impossible to free ourselves. Again we rely on the compassion and competence of Christ in other people.

Who has visited you when you felt imprisoned?

Searching our own experience for the traces of Christ's fingerprints, we may find uncountable blessings. We see that Jesus' incarnation did not occur only once in Bethlehem, but continues right here, right now. When Christ in many faces has helped us so often, how can we turn from him in need? His style teaches us how to "go and do likewise."[2]

God's Precious Diadem

You shall be a crown of beauty in the hand of the Lord,
and a royal diadem in the hand of your God.

—Isaiah 62:3

Perhaps if we thought of ourselves more often as a jeweled band in God's palm, things would go better. We might act more royal and noble in the best sense of those words—not the contemporary corruptions. We could move with confidence through the most difficult situations, knowing we are securely protected. Aware of our inner beauty and price, we might be less inclined to let minor annoyances depress us or major problems defeat us.

Then, with our own health and value firmly established, we could look around at the other jewels in the radiant circle. If we are this precious to God, so is everyone else. It takes the whole lot of us to complete the crown.

It also takes a lot of imperfection transformed. Isaiah's passage about the crown is proclaimed during the Christmas season to show us how completely Jesus' coming changed our status. In his adult life, he sought out the diseased, the lonely, those crippled by a variety of inner and outer ailments. To these in particular he said, "blessed are you."

Not much has changed. In the course of an ordinary week, I encounter four friends in different stages of loss and recognize blessing despite its disguises. One friend is recently widowed; we take a long walk on the first anniversary of her husband's death. She misses the lively conversations about books and ideas, realizes she needs new directions, explores several possibilities. And I marvel at how much raw pain she has survived: a long ordeal with a difficult cancer, the grieving of her children, selling her home and moving, her own loneliness. To a stranger, she might look thin and bent, like one who has suffered much. But I see in her the stamina to survive, the hope for the future, the translucent pearl.

Another friend tackles a college career relatively late in life. Confronting the glossary for the first course, she mispronounces several words and wonders about the meaning of others. She is overwhelmed by the reading list and wonders how she'll ever keep up with younger students. She juggles a full-time job, family commitments, and a long commute. But somehow, she'll make time for school. She isn't afraid to admit her ignorance and do something about it. I admire her chutzpah and commitment; another jewel sparkles.

A third has lost her voice after a virus attacked the vocal cords. It is much more serious than it first sounds. She makes her living by teaching; at the end of a day all she can muster is a coarse whisper. Even worse, she has lost her singing voice, a rich gift and a creative outlet that has enriched many people. She tries to explain the frustration of having a brain that works fine but an essential tool that has suddenly quit. "It's too painful to talk about," she finally concludes about a three-year course of medical treatment. Every now and then, doctors offer a glimmer of hope to which she clings. Beneath the beauty, these are strong diamonds.

A fourth friend has lost her mobility but accomplishes more from a wheelchair than most people with healthy spine and limbs. She explains the philosophy that has underlain her therapy: "Don't think about what you can't do; just find other ways to do it." So she drives a specially equipped van, learns to wrestle with heavy bathroom doors in theaters and restaurants, and struggles mightily with events that most of us routinely ignore.

A quick run to the grocery store? Nope—it's a major trip. A flight to visit her sister? Complexities abound. Supposedly "accessible" buildings? These can entail steep ramps, thoughtless designs, frustrations galore. Yet she lives fully, enjoys her family, gives spiritual direction from the understanding perspective of one who has "been there." A splendid variety marks the dancers of the diadem.

Seeing the faces, knowing the grief of even a few people, we may find ourselves in the position of the magi who made a long journey in search of the savior. They were astonished by what they saw because it ran so counter to their expectations. They did not find a magnificent palace; they stooped to enter a poor hovel. Instead of a powerful ruler, they discovered a baby. But the camouflage of loss did not confuse them long; they were still beneath the sure guidance of the star.

The gospel is terse and does not allow the magi much time to adjust their expectations. Instead, they do the only thing they can in the situation. "Overjoyed," they draw forth their treasure and give it all to the little family. We who have also looked into faces and modified our obsession with appearances must respond the same way. We too pour forth the time, energy, and talents which correspond to gold, frankincense, and myrrh. Knowing our friends or families, we commit to whatever small part we may play in their struggles.

Instinct Becomes Sacrament of Commitment

It seems a purely natural instinct to help out someone who faces an uphill climb. Without going into "team spirit" or military jargon, we intuit that sometimes we're better together than alone. If I can lend the new college student some books or proofread her paper, it enhances us both. If I can push a wheelchair,

I'll gladly give it all the oomph I can muster. Seeing the beauty or need or vulnerability of the other prompts us to bring the union whatever we've got, whether to a community of two or two thousand.

While the scriptural origins of both holy orders and matrimony are iffy, Catholics consider both commitments sacraments. In both ways of life, the sacred permeates the ordinary; the physical points to the spiritual. In the joined bodies of the married couple is the image of God's love for the person. In the touch, the words, the forgiveness of the priest is God's desire to heal, speak to, and nurture God's people. Through both, God's message is loud and clear: *You are not alone in this. It's not just up to you. I'm with you.*

A woman who had recently become Catholic was struck by the promise of a "special grace" conferred by the sacrament of marriage, knowing that it's not meant metaphorically. "According to the sacrament of matrimony, we are now something more than the sum of two shaky human beings occupying the same space and trying to make a go of it."[3] Faith in a marriage, she sees, is not that different from faith in God's inestimable power when invited into any situation.

Murray Bodo, OFM, compares his initial commitment in the priesthood to "a young athlete caught up in the rhythm," an "identification with the ideal."[4] While that might explain youthful dedication, any vocation survives some bitter passages, some downright unholy exiles. Perhaps those are the times of tuition, which convince us that it's not about us—not the marriage, not the priesthood, not the Christian life. It's about the marvels a compassionate God can work in us, no matter our human limitations. And that infusion of the divine in the human, the spirit in matter, the perfect in the imperfect is distinctly sacramental.

Friends

It's 7 p.m. on Thursday, but I can't watch *Friends*. It's usually a Thursday night ritual, one of the few television shows the family ever watches, and we gather round the pseudo-hearth with popcorn or ice cream. A decadent bunch, we snort at the off-color humor and chortle at the zany one-liners. I guess by Thursday, we've given up any pretension of being serious, hardworking sorts.

But this week is different. I've spent my Thursday with friends, the real variety, not the ersatz, made-for-TV model. Instead of phony dilemmas, easily solved in a half-hour with commercial breaks, theirs are genuine and tough.

At lunch four women, political neophytes all, discuss our plans to sponsor an anti-gun-violence seminar. If the churches won't speak out, and the government won't act, then we'll do what we can to stem the insane proliferation of guns. One woman offers the financing, another the site, a third dredges up her political science background from college to interpret documents, another volunteers time for phone calls. We're rookies and we know it, but that doesn't deter us. The cause is just—too many children have died; too many families grieve.

Our burritos are spiced with controversy; our salads seasoned with the gathered energy of the group. We've worked on other unpopular projects; we've confronted the powers-that-be in previous situations; together, we have plenty of combined experience with protests, marches, and demonstrations. An observer might assume that four graying ladies would exchange recipes and pictures of grandchildren at lunch. Instead we unleash tornadoes.

Anointing the Sick

On my way home, I stop by the hospital where another friend's husband lies in critical care. His cancer surgery the day before was a painful, complex ordeal. No one seems to know how long it will extend his life expectancy. My friend is, as I knew she would be, in the waiting room, sound asleep on an upright chair in the middle of noisy chaos. I wake her gently. She explains that she is tired because she spent the night there with a large crowd. They contended for the few couches, and most snored on the floor.

In spite of her exhaustion, she describes her latest theory. Despite billions of dollars worth of high-tech equipment and advanced medical care, people are reverting to the practices of a primitive culture. When one family member goes to the hospital, all go. The hospital is short-staffed, the nurses overwhelmed with paperwork, and some primal instinct prods the family to be there and advocate for one who is sick or sedated.

We talk for a long time, despite the crowd and the uncomfortable chairs. We are more used to conversing on the deck of her mountain cabin or over a glass of Chablis at a neighborhood restaurant. But friendship takes precedence over setting or situation; its unspoken understanding is, "if you must be here, then I will be here too."

We talk of the sublime and the ridiculous—her thoughts on death, the latest crazy news story. We laugh about the "unraveling" of middle age, at the idiosyncratic ways the body falls apart after fifty. More important than any words is the simple act of being together in awful circumstances. If the roles were reversed, she would do the exact same thing for me.

When visiting time is up and my friend returns to her husband, we still feel tired and puzzled. Nothing much has changed in his diagnosis or her sadness. She has no brilliant insights to share with her college-aged children that evening. But in that hour and a half together, something happened that mattered. I could not give it a name until I opened the gospel the next morning to John 15:15. When Jesus described his relationship to his disciples, I could understand it. I'd been there. "I do not call you servants any longer, because the servant does not know what the master is doing; but I have called you friends. . . ."

No one used sacred oils that afternoon, but friendship became a kind of anointing. Months later, I read two questions that could have been asked that day. "What about the anointing, counseling and caring that take time, attention and energy? Must we insist on such a difference between the sacraments and living a sacramental life? One who comforts the sick can anoint."[5]

The writer's experience bore a first-cousin kind of resemblance to mine. While she was arguing for the more traditional anointing of the sick, I had felt part of the strengthening of friends. She too was having a hard time distinguishing between "official seven" and "small s" sacraments. Perhaps the fragrant chrism had blessed us that afternoon after all—unsensed, unguessed—yet falling like balm upon friends.

Commitment Keepers

Son on Highway 25

In one of those complex maneuvers well known to large families with few cars, my younger son and I were returning a car borrowed from my older son. As usual, we were running late, and he roared away in one car with hurried directions to "follow me!" in the other one.

Racing behind, I didn't ponder the irony of his words. In heavy traffic on the highway, I realized I'd lost him during the first five minutes of an hour drive. To make it worse, it suddenly occurred to me that I had only the vaguest notion of how to reach the home of my older son, who had recently moved.

But one line in scripture has always impressed me for its tough femininity. "Who will roll away the stone?" the women ask each other as they approach the tomb of Jesus with their embalming spices (Mk 16:3). Had a committee of men been tackling the same task, I suspect they would have made rules, recruited bull-dozers, brought in the howitzers. The women just keep walking.

So I kept driving. It did briefly occur to me that this was pretty mindless stuff for supposedly educated folk, but I flowed with the traffic as if I knew where I was going. Then, beside me, peering through the window was a freckled face and a grin I knew well. My younger son had surfaced, and quickly took the lead. As his red hair blazed past, I thought gratefully of all the Howdy Doody episodes to which I'd been addicted as a child. Something in the smile was familiar.

At times like that, I want to poke myself. "You were there all along, huh?" I say silently to the invisible companion who also walked with Mary to Elizabeth's, with the women to the tomb, and with two disciples to Emmaus. The prayer of Jesus floats even through twenty-first-century rush-hour traffic: "Father, I desire that those also, whom you have given me, may be with me where I am . . . " (Jn 17:24).

Following Jesus' model, we honor promises to each other in such simple ways, seldom naming them with the high-sounding phrase "sacraments of commitment." Yet as one writer explains, "Sacramentally speaking, God's grace is much too abundant to be left to those in control. Perhaps it is mothers and children who know best how to intercede on our behalf, asking God to give us strength, healing and life."[6]

Volunteers

The promise echoes again through an awards dinner for non-profit organizations throughout the state. The sheer diversity, the prodigious energy of the ventures would impress even the most apathetic. A video celebrates a wide range of projects, all geared not for profit but for help. People do this work not for pay, but to honor a higher commitment, keep a promise which echoes Jesus'.

We see scenes of the blood bank where, immediately after the Columbine shootings, donors waited in line for eight hours to give blood and volunteers worked overtime for two weeks. Then we watch footage of a Native American radio station broadcasting tribal dances and volunteers helping seniors with income tax forms. A center for Alzheimer's patients, a rehabilitation unit for spinal cord injuries, a ranch for at-risk teens, a children's literacy center, an alternate high school, affordable housing, a clinic for indigent toddlers—in all these places breathes a spirit of care.

Surely this world opens a direct door on the next, when it is peopled with so many who look beyond personal gain to the good of others. While the process of canonization in the Catholic church is lengthy, expensive, and political, I suspect that these were the kind of uncanonized holy ones the Persian poet Rumi described:

> Drink from the presence of saints
> not from those other jars.[7]

We are invited to take home the floral centerpieces from the dinner. All week long the aroma of roses fills the kitchen; at every meal we enjoy their dark red petals against a snowy landscape. At another level, it gives us an image of hope: our world is stained by violence and greed, but small pockets of fragrance and beauty flourish through a wintry season. In a hymn of the second century, Hippolytus of Rome praised such abundance: "There's kindness for all to partake of and kindness to spare."[8]

Storyteller

*The day began with reflection on a passage from Thomas
   Merton:*
We live in the fullness of time.
Every moment is God's own good time, [God's] kairos.
*The whole thing boils down to giving ourselves in prayer
   a chance to realize that we have what we seek.*
We don't have to rush after it.
It is there all the time,
and if we give it time it will make itself known to us.[9]

It's probably a consumerist American mentality that
wants to challenge: do we really have *everything* we
seek? What about that mountain cabin or ocean villa?
More talent? Greater compassion? And don't even talk
about the money we wish we had, the great things we
could accomplish with it. But I begin to veer into things
I want or things I'd like. *Seeking* implies activity on a
deeper level, the quest for what nurtures the soul.

It's easier to argue with the statement than do what
it asks: give it time to emerge; give myself time to see
what's been there all along. So the reflection doesn't
end in closure; instead it opens a door to the rest of the
day. Now my curiosity is piqued: if I give it time, will
the day reveal what I've sought without knowing I had
it? As with any good riddle, the answer the day brings
is totally unpredictable.

I'd already planned breakfast with a favorite friend,
whose laughter fills the belly and whose cooking nurtures the soul. As I turn the corner onto her street, I feel
like someone returning to their therapist after a long

stretch. She is a fountain of warmth, vitality, bubbling stories.

We have our ritual breakfast outside on her patio, admiring a floating island of peonies in bloom. Carefully, she shows me the nest robins have constructed in her hanging plant, ignoring the twenty-seven trees in the yard, choosing the basket on the patio instead. Within it nestle four tiny speckled blue eggs.

That discovery is a fitting prelude to her stories. She works with the city's marginalized—addicts, prostitutes, homeless, people struggling to get a GED—and *always* has stories from this world unlike mine. Today she describes a scene where eight mentally handicapped people help at her office on a project for the Peoples' Fair the following week. Her organization's booth will dispense clever "lollipops," condoms on popsicle sticks with catchy slogans like "Safe Sex Is Sweet," "Unsafe Sex Is Sour." The mentally handicapped people can't read the blurbs; they patiently paste what they think are balloons on tongue depressors. All they want in return is hugs, kisses, and assurances; the prostitutes generously oblige.

I think of that scene later at work, and throughout the week. I don't know why it brings such comfort and delight. Perhaps it's the image of folks exiled from every other arena of society, working together, caring for each other on a bizarre project. Perhaps it's imagining "proper folks," eyes rolling and stony gaze averted from such a scandalous scene. Or maybe it's the echo back to the bird's nest—fragile, misplaced, yet still full of life. Most of all it's the tenderness, the unique cooperation of people who aren't exactly on the social registry. I can almost picture Christ pulling up a chair—these are the folks he liked hanging out with!

He also teaches much about forgiveness through my friend. On a recent trip together, I misread the time of our return flight. That miscalculation meant a wild dash to the airport, a process of accomplishing in forty-seven minutes what would normally take two hours. Without a complaint or whimper, she deferred an urgent need to go to the bathroom until we had cleared security. I can admit mistakes to few people, but her broad tolerance makes it easy. In her unregimented reconciliation, Jesus' words take on flesh: "neither do I condemn you."

Bird nest, friendship, breakfast, and stories—Merton was right. The day contained everything I seek, even though I am unaware of what this is. My friend's humor and hospitality carried me through the ensuing hours at the office and home. When the week later became embroiled in rules, regulations, and stultifying restrictions, I returned to the bird's nest as a centered image for the tender care of our God, safely removed from the battle. Even in the midst of controversy, I could turn to other friends for sage advice and solid perspective.

Today I sit at a computer surrounded by pictures, books, and memories, reflecting, trying to capture the immediacy of past experience and tease forth its meaning for the present. Yes, it takes time. And yes, today too, in its own way, has all I seek.

Stranger

On yesterday's walk, I discovered a white fence and an archway covered with morning glories. As the early sun touched the translucent petals, each flower became a little bowl of sky. Such a sight could lift the heart and carry one through the day.

Today I discovered more beauty than morning glories and enough sustenance for several days. A block or two beyond them, I heard the sounds of children screaming, a man's voice yelling, "Shut up!" Unable to place the source, I walked on until I noticed another woman, also out for her morning walk, reversing direction and locating the commotion.

"Sir," she said firmly. When there was no response from the angry man, she repeated it with steel in her voice. Instinctively I went to stand beside her.

It was a typical scene with small children, similar to those in which I'd lost my cool plenty of times. A dad was trying to wedge two kids into car seats in the back of a car. He was probably late for work; they were bellowing and refusing to cooperate. The more he yelled, the more upset they became.

But the unknown woman intervened persistently. "They can't be in control if you're not." She touched his shoulder lightly, encouraged him to take a few deep breaths.

Gradually he regained composure. He was a big man, dressed in work clothes, towering over a small blonde boy and girl.

"You love them, don't you?" the woman asked.

"Oh, yes!" the emotion washed over his face. In grateful relief, he hugged the small but insistent woman who had recalled that fact.

As calm was restored to the scene, she and I continued to walk and talk. Both of us in T-shirts, shorts, and tennis shoes, we were just beginning to realize what havoc we could have stumbled into.

"At first I didn't know what the problem was," she confessed. "I thought maybe he was beating his wife. But thanks for joining me. You never know if they'll shoot you."

"Thank *you*," I replied. "You taught me how to handle a tough situation. You must be a professional."

"Oh no," she laughed. "Maybe we just had strength in numbers."

Or the courage of crazy, convicted people. We never thought of being tomorrow's headline about unmotivated violence, only about intervening on behalf of two children. We had no lofty rationale, just an instinct that sometimes members of a community must take a stand for its vulnerable ones. I'm not a brave sort and rarely consider the duties of citizenship. I'd probably waffle so long before rushing into a burning building that I'd be too late to save anyone. But my hero for today is a nameless woman with ore in her voice, compassion in her touch, and iron in her spine. Three strangers met for a matter of minutes in a random encounter. And the ground beneath our feet was holy.

Theologian Bernard Cooke says that "changing historical circumstances bring new demands of discipleship."[10] Facing difficult decisions, we must wrestle with fitting our own life story into the Christian myth, making our actions correspond to Christ's. "Unless this more basic 'entry into the Christ mystery' does occur, the rituals of baptism and confirmation by themselves are largely meaningless and therefore ineffective."[11]

Initiation into Christ is a life-long process which can occur on a city street with an unknown sponsor. Words like "commitment" may never enter the conversation, and a sacramental link isn't explicit. No one cites the passage, "Where two or three are gathered in my name. . . ." But how can we ever understand the capital S sacraments if we don't live out these surprising lowercase ones?

A Million Moms

She leaves and I feel the same twinge of fear I have felt every morning since April 20, 1999. She goes gladly; she likes her school, Littleton High, located about fifteen miles from Columbine. Her hair is an auburn mantle as she runs into the morning, a clatter of keys, books, and backpack. In the fifteen-year-old world of my youngest daughter, the details are pressing; the larger picture distant.

But Columbine has affected my world, as I suspect it has for many parents. We do not take lightly the hurried goodbye, the last "I love yous" tossed across the quiet morning. It even changes my usual Mother's Day pattern of lounging, planting flowers, enjoying the luxury of a dinner cooked by my four children. Instead, I drive with two daughters to the civic center, crowded with 12,000 other moms, children, and dads. We imagine our gathering replicated around the country, and cheer the figures announced from Washington, D.C.: 500,000 in the Million Moms March there.

I think long and hard about why this gathering seems vaguely sacramental. It is, after all, at Denver's civic center, not its cathedral. Most of the 12,000 people who have gathered wear shorts and T-shirts, not Sunday clothes. Yet this is exactly the purpose for which we were sent forth from church that morning: confront, speak truth, work for justice. A precedent for our activities had been set by a small band of disciples headed into a hostile world, their story recorded in Luke/Acts. A religious conviction drives many of us: that God cares for the vulnerable and confounds the powerful. Enough of us standing together can make a difference and take steps to protect our children from violence.

Many gathered here are veterans of other demonstrations: the civil rights marches, the protests against war in Vietnam and the School of the Americas. Graying liberals, we joke about introducing our kids to the fine subversion of the sixties. But beneath the banter, we recognize that once again the underdogs are tackling the powerful status quo. For the umpteenth time we wonder what one can do against so many. Weakly, we boo the announcement that the NRA will spend $30 million to influence the fall elections. We are up against such wealth, we can only succeed with special grace.

Usually I hate crowds, but today is different. I see materialize what John O'Donohue called community: "It seems that in a soul-sense we cannot be fully ourselves without others. In order to *be*, we need to *be with*. . . . We live such separate and often quite removed lives, yet behind all the seeming separation a deeper unity anchors everything."[12] The film *Choices of the Heart*, about the women martyred in El Salvador, says this in another way: "Alone, we were pretty tough. Together, we were invincible."

Alone, I could never muster the courage to confront the tough reality: the gun lobby has a stranglehold on national and state legislatures. Because of their influence, no significant state or federal legislation was passed in the year after Columbine. Together, however, we have more clout: "Behind all our differences and distances from each other, we are all participating in a larger drama of spirit. The 'life and death of each of us' does indeed affect the rest of us."[13]

These mothers have captured our collective strength in catchy slogans. "Woe to you who try to come between a mother and her child." "Take your gun and go to your room!" "The gun lobby is no match for a million moms." "We love our children more than they love their guns." "Our kids are more protected from an aspirin bottle than from a semi-automatic."

But all the slogans fade before the raw pain of Tom and Linda Mauser, whose son Daniel was killed at Columbine. "Honorary mom" for the day, Tom addresses the group gathered near the capitol where, ten days after the slaughter, he spoke in public for the first time. His words now echo his words then: "I'm here because Daniel would expect me to be here."

Such a simple statement, yet it snags the breath in the throat. I pause in the act of applying sunscreen to my daughter's freckled shoulder. Suddenly the gesture becomes unbearably poignant. I think of all the moms who can no longer do this basic kindness for their children—twelve a day murdered by guns. In Colorado, the litany of names has become a bracelet of memory: Cassie, Steven, Corey, Kelly, Matthew, Daniel, Rachel, Isaiah, John, Lauren, Dan, Kyle, and their teacher Dave.

We know their stories and have memorized their faces. We saw the initial television footage, stunning and stark. The stretchers, the IVs, the sirens, the long procession of ambulances. In shock we endured the irony of funerals where the mourners, the pallbearers, and the deceased were all under eighteen. Now we see the after-effects: the wheelchairs, the surgeries, the rehabilitation that never quite restores the ambling lope of a fifteen-year-old boy, the slender grace of a sixteen-year-old girl.

Perhaps the NRA has met its match. All the money in the world cannot contend with the rage of a mother torn from her child. They have tampered with some deep and primal instinct and they cannot win. An initiative in Colorado required background checks and closed "the gun show loophole." If the legislature could not accomplish such simple measures, the people would. Every mom at that march has a vote—and as we are frequently reminded, a vote is a terrible thing to waste. We may be political neophytes, but we will master any system we must to protect the vulnerable child.

I know with stinging clarity that Lauren or Daniel could have been my daughter or son. My stomach churned when Dawn Anna, Lauren's mom, hugged her slain child's graduation cap and gown and called the valedictorian "a mother's dream." The gun that fired eleven bullets into Lauren was obtained as easily as "taking cereal off a grocery shelf." Despite years of grieving, the stories remain heart-wrenching. I suspect we are ready to take the next step now, make the transition from profound sorrow to vibrant action.

When people feel strongly about an issue, their language becomes direct and dramatic. "Enough," they say. "No more." The anti-gun-violence measures proposed nationally and locally seem mild compared to those of other civilized nations. The statistics are clear, but the joined voice of the mothers roars even clearer.

Listen intently and hear beneath them the tragic moans of students who thought a school library safe. When a community listens hard for God's voice, then its message can mingle divine and human accents. With God's support and in God's presence, we speak God's care: Never again. Never another Columbine.[14]

Lunch Bunch

I admit it: I am rabidly, keenly conscious of time. At long, inefficient meetings, the meter in my head ticks, counting the cost of time dribbled away. I suppose we get this compulsive when we discover that time is more precious than money, and sometimes more scarce. However, an obsession with efficiency sometimes leads us to overlook the ancient distinction between *chronos* (clock time) and *kairos* (God's time).

But a recent experience of the latter—ample, full, overflowing time—revealed the traditional concept in the new and changing contexts of our lives. When we deliberately don't look at our watches, we can discover rare treasure. Let it be recorded then: on September 18, eight of us indulged in a three-hour lunch. There— word is out. Efficiency police to the barricades!

The circumstances leading to this event are less noteworthy than the actual experience, so let's just say we gathered on a warm afternoon. The patio of the Mexican restaurant was peach-colored adobe; the table umbrellas, good and gaudy. The trees around us were lightening into pale yellows; the fountain behind us splashed a watery undercurrent to conversation. The group that gathered was intergenerational; some bare-ly knew each other before lunch.

Everyone there had other pressing agendas. One young couple had just bought a 103-year-old house, desperately requiring renovation before winter. Others had work deadlines; some probably had a "to-do" list lurking in pocket or purse. But by some unspoken con-sensus, we set all that aside.

And we enjoyed each other. Stories rambled over the nachos, enchiladas, burritos, and tostadas.

Laughter punctuated the courses. For that interlude, everyone was, to some degree, witty and charming. As if someone pushed a cosmic "pause" button, time was put on hold. From the fierce pace of twentieth-century urban life, we snatched an afternoon that reminded us what it means to be human in the best sense of the word.

At the time I had not seen Mary Pipher's book *The Shelter of Each Other*. But when I read her praise of such richly idiosyncratic gatherings, I nodded in recognition: "Compared to computer time, everything happens in slow motion."[15]

The next day the weather turned cold and rainy. Chilly drizzle continued for a week, and no one ate outdoors on the patio beneath umbrellas. At the time, we did not think of "mañana," but in retrospect, we were grateful we had seized the last day when everyone wore short sleeves. Such days must be given for our delight, yet how rarely we take the chance to enjoy them. Alice Walker writes in *The Color Purple* that God must get pissed when we walk by purple without noticing. So too God must get annoyed by our workaholic habits. And maybe, when we deviate for a long lunch or a long nap, God smiles.

Because his name appears on so many lists of authors imbued with the Catholic imagination, I reread two of Graham Greene's novels: *The End of the Affair* and *The Power and the Glory*. While some aspects of the faith expressed in them feel stiff as the brocade of another era, his characters ring true. He goes to great lengths to establish their holiness after their deaths, but in life, they are the kind of folks one could comfortably have a drink with. Greene seems to be deliberately contrasting the traditional pious notions of sanctity with real, fleshy saints. In these people "the word becomes flesh," with all the vagaries and glories of skin, muscle, and bone.

In the former novel, Sarah, a woman who toys with belief, visits a Catholic church searching for answers to her questions about God's existence. She hates the bad art, the plaster statues, and "all the emphasis on the human body." It would be easier for her to believe in a God that was "vague, amorphous, cosmic . . . stretching out of the vague into the concrete human life, like a powerful vapour. . . . " But instead she confronts the dramatic reality of the crucified Christ: "I looked at that material body on that material cross, and I wondered how could the world have nailed a vapour there?"[16]

Her parting action as she leaves the church in a rage is meant to flaunt all the tiresome, rational abstractions enshrined by her era: "the Charity Commission and the index of living and better calories for the working class." Instead she does a most Catholic thing, makes a most concrete, material gesture: "I dipped my finger in the so-called holy water and made a kind of cross on my forehead."[17] As Catholics have done for centuries, she grounds herself and her quest in the symbol: water that appears simple, yet contains a wealth of meaning.

Someone reading the story for the first time might naturally cringe with apprehension of saccharine piety. The ending is utterly predictable from the outset. Oh, she'll balk now and then for the sake of the plot twist, maybe encounter a few sufficiently formidable obstacles. But once that train is out of the station, the track is a clean set of parallel lines storming into a soupy, sunset holiness.

Not so with Sarah. For her, coming to faith is no sure formula, but an excruciating leap. Her determinedly atheist lover describes her flaws as well as her launching: "If even you—with your lusts and your adulteries and the timid lies you used to tell—can change like this, we could all be saints by leaping as you leapt, by shutting the eyes and leaping once and for all: if *you* are a saint, it's not so difficult to be a saint."[18]

Sarah is a saint in the Greene pattern: one who surprises God, who steps outside the predictable, trite molds. She refers to herself as "a phoney and a fake"[19] whose adulterous affair is the first step toward God. Through her love for the narrator Maurice, she is drawn into the everlasting arms. While Greene's attribution of three posthumous miracles to Sarah may strain credibility, her own voice nevertheless swells with sanctity. Her complete lack of self-satisfaction or piety exemplifies John's definition of love: "not that we loved God, but that God loved us first" (1 Jn 4:10).

Maurice cannot speak of sanctity in his personal context of disbelief and hatred. So his spare, underhanded compliment dredged out of despair may be an eloquent tribute. "All I know is that in spite of her mistakes and her unreliability, she was better than most."[20]

In *The Power and the Glory*, the contrast between plaster saint and real thing is brought home by the underlying narrative a mother is reading her children.

In this pious *Lives of the Saints*, martyrs die with a flourish, proclaiming: "Viva el Cristo Rey!" Their bravado
heightens the pathos of the whiskey priest's plea: "Do
you have a little brandy?" In his world, everything is
appallingly complex. Not only is he alcoholic, he has
fathered a child. Yet "the sin itself was so old that like
an ancient picture the deformity had faded and left a
kind of grace."[21]

His past is littered with the trappings of religion as
priests who once graced the social scene become out-
casts and fugitives in Mexico. Greene describes how
"feast-days and fast-days and days of abstinence had
been the first to go";[22] then breviary, ambition, and
altar stone become unimportant to a man hounded by
soldiers. As religion leaves the land, it also leaves a vac-
uum; even apathetic Catholics remember the music, the
lights, and the theater—all vestiges of a sacramental
view that are now vanished.

No glory precedes the priest's death, only "an
immense disappointment" that he has done so little
with his life. Then comes an echo of the other novel: "it
seemed to him . . . that it would have been quite easy to
have been a saint. . . . He knew now that at the end
there was only one thing that counted—to be a saint."[23]
After his death, when the children ask their mother if
this exile who "smelled funny" is a saint, she concedes
that he may be, and that it would do no harm to pray to
him.[24]

The symbolism of cock crowing before the priest's
betrayal for a few pesos seems as heavy-handed as the
miracles following Sarah's death. But the bottom line
remains: if these two could be saints, *anyone* could. It
encourages us to look with new eyes at the frustrating
folks who surround us: do vestiges of sainthood lurk
there too? We might even get a jolt of sainthood by
looking in the mirror.

Aerobics Instructor

The new aerobics instructor wore a halter top and tights that gleamed in scarlet spandex. Her voice could be heard in the next state as she announced, "Hi, I'm Mary."

I smiled to myself as I remembered the Marys of my childhood. Quiet and sweet, they gazed demurely at the ground, their hands folded. Everyone's role model then was the Blessed Mother, swathed in blue veils, surrounded by lilies. Her slavish admirers fervently emulated her passivity, her distant serenity. A few girls gave up early, knowing they'd never attain her impossible standard. But the rest of us plugged along, fervently saying the rosary and observing an all-pervasive silence in May.

The futility of that early experience might have led to the wicked pleasure I took in following the aerobics teacher through an intricate routine of straddles, bicep curls, marches, grapevines, crunches, and squats. Rock music blared as our class kept (more or less) the pace of the Rockettes. I wore my leotard with special glee, remembering the yards of red and blue plaid wool uniform that had swathed my skinny twelve-year-old body. From kindergarten through high school, the only movement we perfected was the curtsy, done with the flawless accompaniment of white gloves.

How much healthier it seemed for a group of women to relieve their stress, offset their calories, and whoop it up to teenage music at the end of a work day. We delighted in the feats even aging limbs could perform as we hopped, kicked, and lifted weights. Oxygen coursed through our bodies, clearing our heads and lifting our spirits. Our energy renewed, we swung our legs and circled our arms with more exuberance than we'd ever brought to high school gym class. "How we'd hoot at our former selves now!" I thought—and maybe that's one purpose for high school reunions.

If I attended a class reunion today and met the kind of Mary we idolized in our youth, I'd probably find her boring. I'd tire of her pious blandness after a few minutes of simpering conversation. It warmed my heart to discover scripture scholars who pointed out the grueling distance Mary traveled to visit Elizabeth and the arduous physical tasks demanded of women during her day. "The real Mary could have broken the arms of most artists who depict her as a weakling!" chuckled one.

Another spoke of her influence on Jesus. No wonder he turned out well, with a mother who whispered the "Magnificat" as his lullaby! All that syrupy, unreachable piety was, it seems, the stuff of fantasy. Meanwhile, Mary the Aerobics Instructor barked at us in good drill-sergeant style to *keep moving*! When she'd ask how we were doing, only the most energetic bothered to bleat back. After a chorus of "aaughs!" she'd chirp, "Great! Keep going!"

Since the exercise routine is fairly mindless, my thoughts ranged far. I remembered my friend who uses a wheelchair rejoicing in her children's and grandchildren's unself-conscious use of healthy bodies and strong limbs. I felt grateful that I could jump and run easily, no matter how gracelessly.

And I thought that sometimes we are fortunate when role models shift. In circles where Mary the Mother of God is revered today, it is as God's tender, feminine face. She is the icon of caring, but also of bold courage. Like the sturdy peasant she was, she would probably encourage women's efforts to stay healthy, lively, and connected. Maybe we need a Madonna of the Fitness Center.

PART THREE

Activities: The Hidden Holiness

Because the sacraments are God's self-expression to human beings, and the human celebration of God's presence among us, we cannot consign them to the fringes of our lives or limit them to a few hours in church. Instead we seek the sacramental moment embedded in the ordinary activity, then rejoice when we have found it, like one who finds a pearl, or a treasure buried in a field. When we see that the sacraments are not purely the actions of a priest in a brief celebration, our vision broadens to an ongoing process of recognizing God wherever we are, whatever we may be doing.

Various images suggest different ways to see this hidden holiness. In a reference to John 12:1-8, Susan Ross argues that the sacred cannot be kept bottled in "expensive bureaucratic and clerical jars."[1] Another image proposes rending the veil of the temple so that we can appreciate the beauty of the inner sanctuary. And a dad making lunches muses, "there are seven times seventy sacraments. . . ."

> *If I could give my children my body to eat, again and again without losing it, my body like the loaves and fishes going endlessly into mouths and stomachs, I would do it. And each motion is a sacrament, this holding of plastic bag, of knives, of bread, of cutting board, this pushing of the chair, this spreading of mustard on bread, this trimming of liverwurst, of ham. All sacraments, as putting the lunches into a zippered book bag is . . . even if I do not feel or acknowledge it, this is a sacrament.*[2]

This is a sacrament. How rarely do we name our round of activities like this, yet it could be a constant refrain. It runs through the activities described in these chapters: cooking, exercising, moviegoing, traveling, and enduring a terrible day. The "official" sacraments draw on the most basic human activities—bathing, eating, reconciling, caring for the sick and dying. They are "in turn an invitation to look to others and to the wider world for more signs of God."[3]

As you read this section, be sensitive to the question:

> *Where in your activities do you find a sacramental dimension?*

Then spend some time in reflection or discussion about your activities as sacraments.

Cooking, Eating, Eucharist

Cooking is its own poetry, having certain rhythms and intensities. All the poem's strands culminate in a final stanza that should end with a bang, not a whimper. Its themes come together in a grand finale: Yeats called this the certainty of a box lid clicking shut. So, too, all the feverish work over stove, sink, and refrigerator comes together at the table when hungry folks sit down. Click!

Of course the whole activity is based in splendid metaphor: the giving of life to those we love. In a sense, nothing we do is more important. The sanctity of cooking was recognized long ago by Brother Lawrence:

> *The time of business does not with me differ from the time of prayer, and in the noise and clatter of my kitchen, while several persons are at the same time calling for different things, I possess God in as great tranquility as if I were upon my knees at the blessed sacrament.*[4]

Contemporary people who cook a lot might say much the same thing—if they weren't so frazzled.

Walking in from the office at 5:30 and needing to eat by 6:00 creates a stress that is hardly conducive to contemplation. Maybe that's what drives so many people to guzzle fast food that they know isn't nutritious, and often constitutes a cholesterol assault on the arteries. Maybe because the kitchen *can be* such a pressure zone under such circumstances, we need even more to reflect on its potential as sacred space.

One cook who took time to analyze it (probably *not* between 5:30 and 6:00) talks about turning drudgery to a healing, restorative activity:

. . . partly I think it's the food itself. If you watch, so much beauty passes through your hands—of form, and color, and texture. And energy too. . . . Each grain of rice . . . charged with life and the power to nourish. It's heady, feeling yourself a kind of conduit for the life force![5]

She taps into Carol Lee Flinders' description of cooking: a holy activity, "an enormously rich coming-together of the fruits of the earth with the inventive genius of the human being."[6] Generations have reverenced that process; humans have always drawn close to the table of family closeness, warmth, and the fragrance of food. If only physical hunger were satisfied there, it might be enough. But so many other needs are met: the impulse to process our day even as we repair its ravages and soothe our fatigue.

Of course, cooking is sometimes a matter of grabbing a box of macaroni and cheese; sometimes the warm family sharing disintegrates into a stomach-churning battle. But the aberrations don't have the final word about cooking any more than they do about any other process that can go wrong: parenting, governing, or teaching.

Even a somewhat bizarre cooking experience attunes me more vividly to its potential for joy. In the addled quirkiness that characterizes people-more-attuned-to-ideas-than-daily-realities, I cook on a stove that over the thirty years of its life (well, twenty with us, God knows how many years before that) has gradually lost the broiler, three top burners and the timer. Only when the oven dies do we finally surrender and buy a new one.

We are so amazed by the intervening years of steadily developing oven technology that we gather around as though it were the communal hearth. "Four burners!" one child exclaims. Another runs her hand over the smooth surface which the salesman promises is a breeze to clean. (As if we *ever* cleaned those balky arthritic coils.) We ooh and aah at the timer, the inner light, the nifty broiler. I know—most folks barely blink at these modern developments. Some day, we'll be jaded too. But for now, let's just say that we are slightly strange and it's a novelty.

This shining new presence dominating the kitchen prompts a sudden orgy of baking. One Saturday afternoon, we whip up banana bread, coconut coffee cake, and chocolate French toast—partly for the delight of the yeasty-sweet fragrance in the kitchen once again. For the rest of the week, our youngest daughter invites friends over for a freshly baked snack. They admire the new oven and probably wonder how long they can count on the treats.

Beneath the humor simmers a connection to a larger picture. Kathleen Norris defines resonance: "to resound means to be filled to the depth with a sound that is sent back to its source." It gives the person reading or eating a slice of bread "an emotion made richer by the experience of another."[7] Thus our loaf echoes back in time to another in Palestine over two thousand years ago.

To one who is steeped in the healing, creative work that cooking can be, it comes as no surprise that Jesus chose a meal as the setting for his final hours with his friends. "When you do this, remember me," he said.

Imagine for a moment not knowing the specific context of his words. Think of all the other possibilities to which he might have referred. "When you do this" could have meant healing, teaching, writing, doing the works of justice. If he were a military hero, it might have referred to battle; if he were a civil ruler, it might have meant preserving his laws or policies.

Instead Jesus referred to eating and drinking, activities we do daily and with plenty of scriptural evidence that he did often. His choosing a meal as the context in which to remember him tells us much about Jesus and much about ourselves. It graces not only the last supper, but every meal we eat.

Notice that he and his friends don't troop to the synagogue together; instead they sing psalms over the Passover meal in a home. Jesus knows that the glow of their shared supper will soon give way to the intrusion of torches and the shock of an arrest. He has already voiced his suspicion of treachery fracturing the little circle. Yet Jesus makes his friends a final promise, phrased in terms of a meal: "I tell you, I will never again drink of the fruit of the vine until that day when I drink it new with you in my Father's kingdom" (Mt 26:29). The promise in Mark is similar; Luke's version has: "You are those who have stood by me in my trials . . . you may eat and drink at my table in my kingdom" (22:28-30).

If he had spoken of the glory of heaven and the certainty of salvation, the abstractions might have faded in the brutality that followed. But he gives his friends a concrete image to which they can cling no matter how desperate and depressed they become. Like a frightened child who remembers his mother's kitchen, they can hold on to hope as the image of wine in a cup, a banquet that will surpass any cooking on earth, a home better than any kitchen in this world.

Followers of Jesus continue to find the center of liturgy and life at the table. The subtle message in everything we cook is the same as his: "Come, enjoy. I made this for you. Have seconds!" At every meal, no matter how simple, he joins the circle of affection. Through every morsel we eat, he nourishes. Thomas Merton describes this divine activity interwoven with the human:

> It is God's love that warms me in the sun and God's love that sends the cold rain. It is God's love that feeds me in the bread I eat and God's love that feeds me also by hunger

and fasting. . . . It is God who breathes on me with light
winds off the river and in the breezes out of the wood.[8]

One writer describes the connections between the
altar of church and the table of home. On a typical
Sunday, he teaches religion, attends Mass, then pre-
pares and eats the day's culmination: a "gobs-of-pasta"
early dinner.

I think that dinner is holy. . . . To me it is more important,
at an elemental spiritual level, than Sunday school or even
the Mass, much as I love that miraculous communal theater.
  In fact our Sunday pasta party is a form of respectful, if
loud and bubbly, prayer; and I believe that for us, and per-
haps for all people who believe in God, something like it
is crucial to a rich spiritual life.[9]

"God's joy moves from unmarked box to unmarked
box," writes the poet Rumi.[10] Could it then move like
fragrance from an oven through a kitchen? A simple
family delight becomes part of a longer tradition, mys-
teriously tied to a God who lifted bread reverently in
his hands and admired its tawny crust before he broke
it into the thousand crumbs of his body. What words
could speak to people as directly as this action of feeding, whether the nourishment takes the form of pita or
rice cake or tortilla or brioche or rye?

Bringing Ritual Home

I 'll admit that my work makes me something of a theological junkie, and I have huge admiration for the intelligence and creativity of many theologians. But reading too much esoteric theology has the same effect as breathing too much rarified air. I get the bends. I long for earthiness and example, anecdote and humor.

I start wondering if the authors ever do laundry, water the plants, or have conversations with anyone younger than thirty. They devote earnest attention to ontological mysteries, eschatology, mystagogy, relativism, and post-modernism, but how do they deal with customer service at the phone company? Do they ever wonder whether the deposit will hit the bank before the withdrawal?

An image for this gap between the transcendent heights of most thinkers and the place where most of us live comes from the humorist Bill Bryson. In *A Walk in the Woods,* he describes his adventures hiking the Appalachian Trail. In that remote and isolated wilderness, he admires peaks and forests, but finally concludes, "you can get too much of trees sometimes."[11]

He sums up the American approach to beauty: something you either subjugate ruthlessly, or drive to and deify as holy and remote. In contrast, he recalls hiking through Luxembourg where he spent considerable time in forests, but also delighted in villages, farms, and inns. Beauty in America, he concludes, seems an either/or proposition; seldom do people and nature coexist peacefully. No one understands that "the Appalachian Trail might be more interesting and rewarding if it wasn't *all* wilderness, if from time to time it purposely took you past grazing cows and tilled fields."[12]

There's an analogy here to our way of looking at sacraments. Like isolated mountain peaks, they represent the high points of human life. Beautiful, solemn, wreathed in music, they lift up creation to its original, untainted state—pure as unpolluted water. Language is transformed to song, movement to dance or richly symbolic gesture. These rituals are conducted in the hush of a church where many people dress up. Well done, liturgical celebration can nurture human hunger for the transcendent and give praise to God.

While we appreciate church ritual, we tend to distance it from life, keeping it ensconced with proper ceremony on the high altar. A discreet "don't touch" sign proclaims the liturgy off limits to grubby children, feisty women, and the unordained. Speaking of the rituals and shrines people have created closer to home, at Columbine, Oklahoma City, and ground zero, Richard Rohr writes:

> There are monuments of remembrance in front of every city hall and rituals of joy and renewal by fringe groups on every spring and summer solstice. We dare not laugh at them. If we will not rightly celebrate the true heroes and paschal seasons, then the very stones must cry out.
>
> People are inherently sacramental. They know no other way to make sacred their fragile lives except through ritual, song, symbol, prayer and holding human hands. This is how they let God touch them. Precisely when the patriarchs are forgetting how to do it, ritual is being picked up, often in crude and clumsy form, by feminist circles, bereavement, justice and minority groups and belief systems of every stripe.[13]

What if, like Luxembourg, we were to draw the sacraments closer to our daily lives? Not that there won't always be a place for solemn ritual, just as there will always be places where casual dress won't cut it. (Indeed, those who've attended rambling, folksy weddings or funerals attest to the painful embarrassment that can ensue when ritual is neglected at a time that demands solemnity.)

But what if we saw more clearly the links to ordinary reality? An alpine trail is no less beautiful because it loops around a cow pasture; indeed, a moo or two can liven up a silent hike. So it is not irreverent to draw the sacraments into closer contact with daily experience. Rather than relegating them to a distant library, it enriches us immeasurably to bring them closer to the kitchen.

Perhaps a few examples may clarify this direction. A mother of a severely handicapped child writes of sewing her daughter's first communion dress. The seams of white eyelet "closed old wounds" and helped piece together a faith that had become lost in the anguish of a terrible diagnosis. With any luck, the doctors had said, Laura would live to be three. Her mother comments: "When she was eight, we knew we were on borrowed time."

When a sympathetic catechetical director invited Laura to receive first eucharist, her delighted mother began to sew the white dress. "The bedroom became a sacred space, the sewing of the dress a sacramental creation. It was a time of inner transformation and conversion."[14]

Anyone who thinks that such homey celebrations are only the province of women needs to revisit Thomas Merton:

psalms of the rain,
of the odors and crackling of the fire,
the psalms of the stars and the clouds and the winds in
    the trees—all equally eloquent.
And also in this context,
the psalms of one's coughings and sneezings and coffee
    drinkings.
The psalms of one's heat rash—
for in this nothing need be hidden from God,
and nothing is lower than any other thing.[15]

Contemporary environmentalist Thomas Berry adds:

In everyday Catholic terms, think about our educated sense of what is "holy." For the most part the sanctuary of the church was presented to us as a sacred place, whereas that grove of sycamore trees down in the park, full of the magic play of light, shadow, aromas and refreshing breezes was not, until recently, considered a place where God was especially present. The priest was on the inside track to "holiness" while parents and neighbors were down the list.[16]

Those who are not yet convinced need only face a time in their lives which calls for a ritual not included in the church manuals. Sending the first child off to kindergarten or the last one off to college, moving from one home or apartment to a new one, graduating, retiring, packing up the belongings of one who has died, divorcing, receiving a terminal diagnosis: where in the *Sacramentary* do we find the appropriate words, symbols, and rituals for these life-changing events?

Transforming

Winter Landscape

The landscape in early March is bleak—the trees still skeletons, the ground bare and brown. In other climates, daffodils may bloom and crocuses emerge, but not here in Colorado. Not yet.

This morning we wake to find a heavy snow weighing down the evergreens, softening the gables of the house across the street, whitening the ground. It falls steadily all day and the landscape is transformed. A spring snow doesn't affect road conditions as adversely as one in December or January might; it melts quickly. Without worry over cancellations and accidents, we can simply enjoy the beauty.

The snowfall coincides with the second Sunday of Lent, when we hear the story of Jesus' transfiguration. For a few moments on a mountaintop, Peter, James, and John beheld Jesus' shining glory that at other times was veiled. Even a glimpse of his radiance made them want to set up house and stay.

The snowfall and the story coalesce with two other events of my week, and I am learning that when events converge like this, it isn't mere coincidence. Earlier that week, I had heard Wayne Muller, author of *Sabbath*, speak. His topic was the Big Questions that should engage us more than a preoccupation with answers. The first one he posed was, "Who are you?"

At the easiest level, most of us would respond, "mother/father, spouse, sibling, daughter/son," and characterize our profession. But the question has a way of probing deeper. One answer might be "I am one who is being transformed."

The Person Transformed

At a funeral later in the week, that question and answer took on flesh. We celebrated the life of a Jesuit priest who in his early adulthood was a handsome athlete, the kind of person who was put in charge of many things, a bright achiever. In the last ten years of his life, however, a series of strokes and surgeries took away his stature, his mobility, his health, his speech, and his short-term memory. His life had taken on the contours of St. Ignatius' prayer: "Take, Lord, receive: all I am and possess. My memory, my understanding, my entire will. . . . Give me only your love and your grace: that is enough for me."[17]

So some might have referred to him as a stroke victim, or a helpless hospital patient. But we who gathered in his memory saw differently. Over and over, people spoke of the light in this man. If someone had asked, "What kind of God do you have?" we could've pointed to our friend as one window on a deity who is "slow to anger and abounding in kindness." Despite his own pain, this priest greeted every request, every suggestion the same way. "Great!" he'd say, and repeat it for emphasis: "great! great!"

Through a long and arduous process, our friend had been transformed. Asked "Who are you?" he would no longer respond, "dean of the university," or "pastor of the parish." Such terms were too small for him. The only answer approximating truth would be "light of the world."

So are we all engaged in a process of transformation. Grace falls as steadily and softly upon us as the snow over the landscape. We probably aren't even conscious of the many ways we are being shaped into the image of the creator. We could no more point to the steps in our slow molding than the tree could show the difference in snow-covered limbs, or the ground describe the difference in its texture or tone.

Sometimes a good friend can show us, or a stranger's comment highlights some facet of ourselves that no one would have noticed five or ten years before. Sometimes random comments can testify to great change, which we ourselves are the last to notice. In this way, I guess the snow is sacramental, suggesting human growth in the only way it can ever happen—through mystery.

Easter Egg Hunt

When the outer world mirrors the inner, we see transformation on a larger stage, surrounding us. Just over a month later, April brings another enchanting transformation. The trees flower in pink-white clouds of dogwood and apple blossom; the birds sing an alleluia chorus. The grass is lush and green, shimmering with dew nested in the long blades. For once, I do not envy people who live in the perpetual summer of Florida or California. They miss the seasonal transition from winter to spring.

In our house, the pinnacle of spring is the Easter egg hunt. Our children bring friends home from college for the event, and even the college graduates wouldn't dream of not participating. The rest of the year (except Halloween), we aren't big candy eaters. But Easter provides a religious excuse! The Mother Bunny hides the candy all over the yard in devious and sneaky places, a painstaking, time-consuming process usually wiped out in a matter of minutes.

During those minutes, the world is the way every child dreams it. Briefly and fleetingly, every branch glimmers with foil wrappings; every leaf conceals a tiny egg, the dumbest rock holds a surprise, and every nook of porch, swing, or fence hides treasure. Over the scene sway flowering boughs and the air itself is scented. The children and young adults running with baskets into the spring morning are seeing the world with enchanted eyes. Everywhere lurks the sacred, and the golden

Cadbury egg may appear just behind the log or around the gate.

Our religious sensibility finds grace everywhere, permeating the most ordinary objects, people, places, and activities, but here it is most obvious. Later that day will come the negotiating, trading the mints for the caramels, but during the whirlwind of Easter morning, we enter fully into play and delight. It becomes a microcosm for a larger life.

Later that morning when things have quieted down and the children settle into a sugar-induced stupor, I have more time to reflect. Just as the Jewish writer Ettie Hillesum once internalized the flowering jasmine, I meditate in the presence of a flowering cherry tree. As St. Francis de Sales wrote, "We pray best before beauty." I feel a bit like the squirrel in its branches with the mouthful of blossoms, petals hanging from whiskers. Does he taste the fruit in the flower?

Surely for a human, this Easter tree at its peak, exploding in white froth is a clear symbol of God-with-us, God who is Beauty. A line from Beatrice Bruteau makes the perfect accompaniment to the scene. She explains the significance of the Incarnation: we believe that we can be with God, in God. Our life, taken up and joined with God's, responds to the invitation of Jesus: "This day, be with me in Paradise" (Lk 23:43). She comments, "surrounded and permeated by the glory of God's own joy, how can we care for, even notice [other] ways of valuing our life?"[18]

At the center of our hearts, deep in the core of our being, lies a hidden bliss. It comes from God and longs for God. When we are quiet enough to listen to it we know we are made for eternity. Even though its flowering is brief, the cherry tree, with puffs of white against blue canopy filled with song, symbolizes eternal bliss.

"We want more from religion now than rules. We want something to help us find meaning in life when all the rules cease to make sense, when all the old systems break down or fade away. We want a glimpse of God here and now," writes Joan Chittister. Now and then, we get a glimpse—in snowfall and cherry tree, in human life transformed.

Traveling

Sometimes travel helps me understand the sacraments of the world. One spring Saturday I'd been skiing on the high mountain peaks of Breckenridge. The day was filled with abundant powder, warm weather, and clear skies over radiant mountains. At the end of the day, we had a good soak in a hot tub, pizza for dinner, and a deep sleep beneath a down comforter. The condominium where my daughters and I stayed was artistically furnished, complete with fireplace and balcony overlooking a mountain view and a valley snuggled in purple shadows.

If this all sounds a bit idealistic, perhaps it was. But I wanted my younger daughter to have, at least for a couple days, the perfect start to her spring break. Perhaps guilt was at work too—I knew I'd be leaving the following Saturday and wanted to make our time together special. Which it was for me. I carried the memory like a little jewel on my flight to the east coast the following weekend.

Bear in mind that writers exaggerate because sometimes only drama can make the point. Some eastern cities are beautiful, and I have had splendid times in the East with wonderful people. But this city was dreary. To make it worse, my lodging for the weekend was furnished in depressing shades of brown. The place was full of furniture, all monstrously large, so dwarfing me that I felt I'd swallowed Alice in Wonderland's shrinking potion.

Arriving late, I spent a sleepless night in an uncomfortable bed. When I awoke to the view of a cemetery outside my window, it seemed an ominous sign. I missed the balcony overlooking the mountain vista. In the hazy fog and drizzle, I longed for Colorado sunshine. Most of all, I wondered how Jesus endured the journey from the shining radiance of God's reign into a backward corner of the world that must have seemed bleak by comparison. I tried to do what he did: seize on what was beautiful and life-giving.

Lifting good things to our clouded vision, Jesus said, "the reign of God is like this." He held up what was best in a disordered world and taught about God from it: vines and branches, rising dough, lampglow, birdsong. Rarely did he dwell on laws or rules; instead he invited, "consider the lilies of the field." Perhaps he focused on the things that reminded him of home.

So I followed his lead, grateful for a fruit bowl kindly placed in my room, with the red gleam of apple, the sweet juiciness of orange, the pale green globes of grapes. Later at church, I noticed a song well sung, the brilliant jade of trees brushing the stone walls outside.

We who know human love through sensate actions—the work undertaken, the compliment voiced—know divine love in the same way. Without such signs, how would we know of God's bold, fierce love? Yet even the sign can be ambiguous and incomplete, not only revealing God, but also concealing God's presence. Like the human gesture of affection, it beckons us to more: one hint makes us want more contact, more time, more of the beloved.

If someone in that eastern city had never visited Colorado, how would they know what it was like? I would muster my best pictures and descriptions to capture the piney air of a mountain morning, the sunset gilding a peak, and the streams like sheets of water. It wouldn't be as good as a plane ticket, and couldn't substitute for the direct experience, but the small signs would do for now.

That morning at church I discovered a lovely image for this translation that Jesus tried to do. The area behind the altar was painted in the same shade of brown (they must've gotten a discount) and the homily was mediocre. But when the priest began the eucharistic prayer, he suddenly broke into sign language. A cascade of lovely gestures fell eloquently against the backdrop of his purple vestments. Such poetry in his hands!

Then it struck me: so Jesus learned our language. Stunted as it must've been, he found the highlights and used them to speak. Snagged by compassion for us, he directed our focus to what is finest in human life and said, "You can learn from this. Better yet, you can find me here." So he gave us a language of places and persons and activities and things where we might find God. Peter Maurin and Dorothy Day, creating the Catholic Worker movement, wanted a world where it would be easier for people to be good. So God gave us one.

After a couple days in which I grew to like the people and the environment of this anonymous eastern city, I boarded a plane bound for Colorado. I was filled with elation; the white mountains beckoned. At that moment, I understood a passage in John's gospel: Jesus, knowing "that he had come from God and was going to God . . . " (13:3) washes the feet of his disciples. His life was bracketed securely—beginning and end firmly placed in his Father.

What was true for him is true also for us. Knowing that I came from the beauty of Colorado and would return there, I could endure and even enjoy the eastern sojourn. I could eagerly describe my home for others who hadn't visited. Knowing that we come from God and return to God, what more do we really need on earth? Maybe the signs between the brackets for reminders, the "small s" sacraments.

Keeping Sabbath

For a week or sometimes longer, we walk around blind or lame, hardly noticing the limp. But by the time the weekend approaches, we need healing. We are drained, exhausted, bent beneath pressure, crabby, and short on time. Physical and mental illnesses often get scrambled, and without any formal diagnosis, we know we're sick. Perhaps we're not seriously ill, nowhere near hospitalization, but lacking the energy and zest to start another week. One reason we keep Sabbath is for its healing touch. We approach Sunday rituals like the walking wounded, desperate for a cure.

For some folks these rituals occur in church, and at our house formal worship will come later in the day. The earlier hours bring a healing ritual that fills me with peace and security. It is the one morning that we can sleep late. Late means 9 a.m., an indolence fully appreciated only by those who have been up at 6:00 every other day of the week. On Sunday, we plunge sleepily into the morning grayness as into a pool of restoration.

My consciousness fades in and out like shadows on a hillside or clouds above a lake, sometimes hazily awake, sometimes dreaming. The usual hard, fast lines and boundaries fade away. I drift in and out of sleep like a loosely anchored boat on an undulating sea.

My husband's arm around me keeps me warm; his deep breathing wraps me in an easy rhythm. I wish I could say that for the thirty years of our marriage we have cherished this ritual, but for many years a baby's cry pierced the morning, or toddlers demanded an early breakfast. Only as the offspring grow older can parents nest in snug peace.

As my husband awakens slightly, he rubs my shoulders and back. Unconsciously he responds to the lines of Irish poet Seamus Heaney: "Attend. Anoint the wound."[19] He does not know all the tensions he soothes, nor all the reasons why the stress has accumulated in my neck. But he wipes it away, as I do for him, cleaning the slate for another week.

Perhaps the greatest relief of this ritual is knowing there is absolutely nothing we must do. If we choose to lie here and listen to the enveloping rain, we can. If we drift back to sleep, that's okay too. For people who are overly responsible and usually coping with a full schedule, the absence of demands is bliss. We begin to understand why God "provides for his beloved as they sleep" (Ps 127:2, NJB).

When I am traveling, Sunday morning does not have such pleasant connotations. It usually means get up early, pack bags, and drive to the airport, or give a workshop. Missing the ritual now and then only heightens my appreciation when I return. Nowhere else can I sleep so deeply, dream so well, or snuggle so completely into the essence of "home." This Sunday comfort hints at the promise in John's gospel: "we will come to them and make our home with them" (14:23).

The root meaning of the word "sabbath" is to separate. This day clearly delineates one week from another, and not so clearly marks the dividing line between work and play. In other eras, that distinction might have been clearer—a day off from the mine or the factory was indeed a time to celebrate. For us the difference may be more psychological than physical. On Sunday we can hunker down into family and home, postponing anxiety 'til Monday morning.

Donna Schaper describes this pause to remember what is holy in both work and play. "It is not that our work is not holy or that our play necessarily is; rather, our days nest in levels and layers of holiness."[20] Sometimes we are so full of tension, there's little room left in our minds or hearts for God. On Sunday, the stress can ebb away. Relative calm and rest can re-create a space for God.

For every hundred people, there are probably a hundred ways to "keep holy the Lord's day" and heal the self battered by the week's demands. One friend cherishes a Sunday morning ritual of donuts, milk, and the *New York Times*. Another cooks a huge dinner; a third takes a long walk outdoors. Each person knows from experience what restores energy and peace after a hectic week. In this activity, they find one of the "chancels that humanize humans," a restorative ritual that in all its essentials echoes the anointing of the sick.

Sometimes, too, the ritual resonates with dying: we look back over the week's losses, great and small. Perhaps we say goodbye to unrealistic expectations: I'll never be president, pope, or CEO. The house isn't immaculate and the bank account isn't overflowing. We give up our delusions of greatness and ease more happily into who we are—limited but loved.

We find some of the same components in gospel stories of healing. Oddly enough, Jesus' curing on the Sabbath sent the religious authorities into a special frenzy. He answered his attackers with perfect priorities: "The sabbath was made for humankind, and not humankind for the sabbath" (Mk 2:27).

We meet him here as the people of Palestine once did: through warm touch, words which dismiss guilt, questions inviting our active engagement in the process, "what do you want?" Then we answer in our different ways: I really need help in this relationship/ I'm over my head at work or school/ I can't bear to see my parent suffer/ I've lost my patience with the children or coworkers.

From the Sunday rest, we go forth restored, perhaps not completely but in some small degree. Like Lazarus, we are called from sleep into the unknown, but our names are called by one who loves us. We enter the next week renewed to serve.

Enduring a Terrible Day

By now Judith Viorst's classic book for children has slipped snugly into the lingo. Who hasn't suffered with Alexander a "terrible horrible no good very bad day"? A list of precisely what that entails seems like overkill: everyone can jump in with a personal version.

Let's just sum it up by saying that the voice of creation which often speaks to us of God falls deafeningly silent. Somewhere the sunset ignites the western sky, a couple reconciles or a new-mown lawn smells fresh and sweet—but in the Funk, we don't much care. The soothing efforts of friends and family miss their mark. We growl at jokes that would usually make us chortle. The more neurotic tend to mentally replay the details of our (check one)

- ❏ humiliation
- ❏ rejection
- ❏ glaring mistake

like a VCR stuck on rewind.

Where is God when everything goes wrong? If we hold that God dwells in all things, then might God not enter the blizzardy day as well as the balmy one? Do 128 miles of road construction pose a serious obstacle to the Creator of the universe?

Some might say that our frustration with the (check one)

- ❏ computer
- ❏ boss
- ❏ bank

❑ spouse

❑ car

❑ coworker

❑ child

is more our problem than God's. But to think that God looks discreetly away as we throw a temper tantrum is to deny that God is intimately involved in the prickly details of our lives. To assume God doesn't care misrepresents the deity Jesus imaged as a woman (herself having a bad day) who overturned her household to find one lost coin.

To understand how God might affect the gloom, an insight from theologian Susan Ross might be helpful. She reminds us that the sacraments not only reveal God, they veil God. Because nothing can capture the full wonder of the deity, they are incomplete messages, unfinished symphonies. They may *point* to God, but they are not God. Because they arise from an ambiguous human world, they are also ambiguous.[21] They speak of a God who is not only immanent (intimately engaged with humans) but also transcendent (way beyond us).

To truly reflect the human condition, the sacraments cannot stand apart and distant from our often confusing realities. If they do become too perfect and sophisticated, they grow too far from their roots in complex, messy human experience.[22] The eucharist, for instance, is a sign that motley, marginalized people, some with headaches and others with depression and still others carrying unresolved rage, can dine peacefully at the same table. Such inclusion signals that God welcomes *all* of ourselves (the part that cruelly wounded a dear friend as well as the more stellar parts) to God's banquet. Who, then, are we to berate and condemn ourselves? The only blockades to God are those we humans build.

While we have tended to see God in beauty and order, the Dreadful Day brings us to the uncertain spaces where change and transformation can occur, however painfully. Sometimes when we teeter precariously in chaos we grow significantly—but we should probably not point that out, however kindly, to one still stuck in the morass. After repeated Bad Days, we may learn new ways to seek the God beyond.

If we go back to the principle underlying all sacraments, God is revealed in the world, not apart from it. For example, think close to home, of the family which can be our most intimate, loving, supportive sphere—or a hell hole where we are tempted to strangle our nearest and dearest. If such mysterious ambiguity marks our closest circle, it must carry over to all creation.

Perhaps part of our growth is developing the ability to move beyond the signs which often speak so eloquently of God. On some days, we simply don't receive those signals. For whatever reason, we are cut off from the flow of sensate messages that usually speak to us of God, a phenomenon the saints called "the dark night of the soul." Those who endured it found that the only path through the experience was to step outside their chattering minds and into God's deep silence. Whether we image God's heart as a safe harbor, warm hearth, cool shade, or tender embrace, its inner peace awaits when the outer signals dim.

Exercising

Q: Is God here, even in aerobics class?
A: Is God everywhere?

What I learn at the gym probably doesn't compare with what I learned in kindergarten, but it points to a divine dimension in the ordinary routine. Surely God is present where I find such richness:

1. The Kindness of Strangers

The women in aerobics class aren't the ones with whom I work, chat on the phone, or go to lunch. If I ever saw them out of their sports togs, I probably wouldn't recognize them. Yet we enjoy the camaraderie of strangers. Usually on similar schedules, we attend the same classes and for three hours a week create the local YMCA version of *Riverdance*. Together we thump, jump, laugh, do modified jumping jacks, yelp, and whine.

Our exercise together corresponds vaguely to Weight Watchers or Alcoholics Anonymous. Nobody's perfect but everybody tries. In silent compact, everyone avoids mentioning that middle-aged women look bizarre in neon shorts and that spandex only accentuates the cellulite. The other Great Unspokens center on our being woefully out of shape, usually out of step, and often out of sync.

If someone slips or falls, the etiquette prescribes that those in the immediate neighborhood ask calmly, "You OK?" With utmost courtesy, they then continue neglectfully on. No one ever makes enough fuss for the fallen one to feel like a klutz. Some of the more exquisite comments ascribe blame to shoes or equipment—never to the real cause, the exerciser.

Some mysterious principle provides that the older people get and the more they exercise, the more relaxed they become. It's only the newcomers who are nervous, and after a few months of sweaty duds and sloppy T-shirts, they fit right in like normal folks. For a support group without bylaws or nametags, it works pretty well.

2. The Importance of Paying Attention

Aerobics class reinforces my preference for experiential learning over any vicarious form. This is one classroom where it's impossible to sit passively; everyone is actively involved. (When my pastor once complained that the parish hosted more aerobics classes than Masses, I suggested that he examine why. Maybe people prefer being involved, no matter how imperfectly, I hinted. Maybe they're tired of watching in a spectator stupor while one man does almost everything?)

It also forces me to focus, because not doing so has serious consequences. If my attention drifts to rewriting a poem in my head, I'm likely to miss a beat or a direction, or more likely, land on my noggin. However bizarre the movements seem, they are all-absorbing. While I've read books about being aware and heard talks about living in the present, this activity forces me to do so—or else.

3. The Ease of Recovery

Those who've been at this the longest develop a whole repertoire of compensatory mechanisms. So you miss a step? Wait for the next one. Turn left when you should turn right? Soon enough everyone else will be on your page. Miss a whole sequence? Catch up when you can—everyone else is concentrating so hard on their own workout, they don't much care about yours. Aerobics, like life, is full of second chances. Rarely is a misstep fatal. And the race, in the long run, may be won more by the persistent than the swift. Physical rhythms have much to teach the mind—so sometimes we just need to relax and let the bodily memory take over. Maybe it teaches us to be more forgiving about our own failings—and those of people around us.

4. The Value of Play

Adults look silly counting jumping jacks or frowning intently to get that "mambo-cha-cha" down pat. Perhaps taking it seriously undermines the whole purpose of play. To those who are sweating and grunting, the instructor's casual "having fun?" sounds sadistic. But when *else* during the week do we have an hour for music, motion, and not a single important decision?

The woman who is concerned for at least seven other hours of her day with the NASDAQ or the latest techniques of cranial surgery focuses intently on the hamstring curl. (Those who don't concentrate on their diagonal pivot will find themselves in the aforementioned, awkward position of the crashing klutz.) Most of us probably don't take our hip flexors seriously enough, but if the body gets its due, its daily hour, it seems to cooperate better in our brainier schemes.

Scientists could explain the role of endorphins, but refreshment must be one purpose that brings many folks to the gym. For an hour they set aside everything, and return to it better able to cope. With the stress worked out and the body energized, we can almost shout, "Bring on the work!"—and almost mean it. One reason we run or row, dance or swim may be to rediscover the pleasures that children find in play. If, as many traditions believe, the body is a temple for the divine spark, it's a spiritual practice to take care of it.

5. Attitude Is Everything

Even a casual observer can see several distinct styles in an aerobics class. Some are obviously trudging through, working off the calories, heavy with guilt over the turtle cheesecake. Others are still trying to figure it out; "clueless" would be the kindest description. (To look awkward in this group takes some doing!) Others are dancing with delight, glad to swing their arms and legs in loops and arabesques. They were probably the kids who swung gracefully across the monkey bars, but this is no time for envy.

In a sense, the workout is a microcosm of the larger world. How many times have we seen a child explode with wonder over an unusual bug in the grass as a jaded adult yawns in boredom? At the end of a marvelous skiing day, when the snow was powdery, the weather warm, and the sky blue, I overheard the young couple next to me at the lockers complain, "That was horrible! What a waste of money and time! We're *never* coming back here!" Had we been at the same place all day?

The third-century philosopher Marcus Aurelius may have explained the discrepancies. "The color of one's thought dyes one's world," he said. Some must see the world in drab monotones, while for others it sings in brilliant shades. Perhaps the sacramental imagination enters here. Those who approach the day like a gift-wrapped box know it contains some challenges as well as treasures. But they also discover, as did writer Frederick Buechner: "Needless to say, church isn't the only place where the holy happens. Sacramental moments can occur at any moment, any place, and to anybody. . . . If we weren't blind as bats, we might see that life itself is sacramental."[23] Exercise as a vehicle for grace can fit that description and qualify as a "small s" sacrament.

Detouring

"God loves to look at us, and loves it when we will look back at him."[24]

But how seldom we look back. Perhaps that's why I pause in the midst of a busy week and pull out of rush hour traffic into a little park. I've been here before; the walking paths are familiar. As I follow one that parallels a stream, the burbling noises drown out the traffic roar, reduced by distance to a low purr.

There's something almost patriotic about those droves of people driving downtown. They look serious and responsible; they ponder decisions and schedules on their way to work. The message is almost engraved on their foreheads: "We have jobs. We support the economy. We are the pillars of society."

I can't get too sarcastic about them, because I will soon join the crowd, drive to my office, park in the garage, and ascend the elevator with everyone else. Then I will engage in work that is more or less boring, livened now and then by a phone call, an e-mail, a donut, or a coworker's joke.

But not yet. For now, I move through a world of leaves on stately trees and waters calmly mirroring sky. It is a lovely place, and the deeper I enter into it, the more I think about looking at God. How much is written on the faces we lift to God, how much God sees. Yesterday, there was anger; I'd just heard about an incompetent boss getting a ten percent raise while a marvelous employee got none and quit. On the scale of injustices, that's a minor blip, but one look at the morning paper would give more ammunition: war, refugees, disease, flooding, and hurricanes dominate the news.

So the face I turn toward God bears the marks of anger and confusion. The all-seeing Creator would also notice sadness there. For I'd dreamt about a friend I'd once been close to, but we had drawn apart. In the dream I asked, "After we have had so much together, how can we now be silent?" Surely there was a way to mend the breach, but I had to think through how.

I also mused on a woman in a group I'd spoken to last week, who burst into tears as she told me about her nine-year-old son, recently diagnosed with diabetes. Or the young neighbor, a teacher who had just given birth to a son with Down syndrome. How could I speak to either woman of God's delight without insulting their sadness?

Such thoughts shadowed my steps, but the further I walked into beauty, the deeper I breathed crisp air, the more I realized that the positive and negative could walk along together, in the rhythm of two hiking feet or two swinging arms. Not that the answers came in a flash, but that I could more comfortably accommodate the questions. Then the face I lift to God can contain joy and gratitude, along with outrage and perplexity.

Maybe that's why I turn off the highway into the little park on the way to work. Kathleen Norris knows my purpose better than I do: "to let ourselves look at God, and let God look back at us." How much is contained in a look, how much living wrapped into the silence, how much experience weighed and measured in a twenty-minute walk.

Attending a Retirement Dinner

When a hundred and twenty teachers retire from a large public school district, appropriate ritual honors them. Corsages and boutonnieres, a gracious dinner, the high school madrigal singers. Someone has calculated their 1,840 combined years of service to children: an average of twenty-three each.

But the full impact doesn't hit until a video opens with scenes of the early seventies: impossibly old cars parked before spanking new buildings. The young district is expanding and teachers are hired right out of college. The men have longish hair and big collars; the women, fresh-faced and eager, are surrounded by kids. They were new, energetic teachers poised on the brink of a career. Their youthful pictures are then juxtaposed with current photos. Time has brushed the faces; the hair has turned gray or white; the years have swept like winter over slim bodies and erect postures.

The pictures are silent witness to twenty-three years of getting up every morning, even in cold, dark February, to countless children—the difficult ones and the rays of light, the inevitable struggles and the quiet, hidden rewards. These teachers have tried new techniques, attended a lot of in-services, corrected more papers than they care to remember, and rejoiced in summer vacations. They are a tribute to human endurance and should be serenaded by angel choirs. Instead they receive a handshake from the superintendent, a plaque, a photo, and it's all over, a twenty or thirty-year career ended in a blink.

The ramifications are still unclear, because they remain embroiled in end-of-year routines. One conscientious retiree confesses that she's been late returning fourth-grade papers—after several parties, she's been busy writing thank-you notes. "The children wanted them back Monday, but they won't get them 'til Wednesday," she whispers conspiratorially, as if confessing to ax murder. I respond in kind: "So what can they do—fire you?"

No one denies there will be a transition, but the retirees seem filled with plans, buoyant with possibility, dizzy with the thought of all that free time. They are off to Ecuador, Nepal, cabins in the country, and trout streams. They will read as late as they want and sleep in. They have spent the coinage of their youth on children's education, a noble enterprise in a fine district that paid them well, honors them now, and rewards their retirement. One could do worse.

As an observer, I know this experience is given for a reason, for more than platitudes about time's swift passage and the reverence due each day. So I muse: *Maybe when "God has a dream for you" it's not Hollywood glamour. Maybe after you live it out, you walk a little slower and your hair turns white and you wrinkle and gain weight and bend a little. But you also gain confidence, grace and skills you lacked in youth. You carry a lot more people in your heart. You treasure your time because you know how quickly it goes and your children because they grow up fast. "You will bear much fruit and in you my Father is glorified. . . . " Fruit could look like lesson plans and carnivals and field trips and art projects and parent conferences and math problems and snacks. It could be the glow on the face of the retiring teacher whose superintendent hugs him and says, "It's been a great ride!"*

In God's dream, nothing is ever lost. The Jesuit poet Gerard Manley Hopkins in "The Leaden Echo and the Golden Echo" encourages us to "give beauty back to God" who will preserve it better than we can.

When the thing we freely forfeit is kept with fonder a
*   care,*
Fonder a care kept than we could have kept it, kept
Far with fonder a care (and we, we should have
*   lost it). . . .*[25]

When God starts dreaming for you, look out. You pour out your youth and affect the lives of children. You go to a retirement dinner, get misty-eyed, and come away a little changed. Maybe you see how the work of teachers constitutes a "small s" sacrament.

Flying

Maybe I'm a sucker for the honey-roasted peanuts. Or perversely, I enjoy the race between a bladder full of Diet Coke and the pilot switching off the Fasten Seat Belt sign.

Or maybe it's more. Maybe I like chasing the sunset on a west-bound flight, thinking the day will never end and the horizon will always be smudged with crimson. Flying east, I'm the one in the window seat, watching dawn tint the sky pastel. I'll abandon my book to watch in fascination as back-lit clouds coil up like mountains and the blue shadows between them nestle like lovely valleys. Texas skies in particular have pillars and billows and sculptures of clouds, scarves and shreds of chiffon against blue silk.

Perhaps I like the perspective gained only from the air. When the light falls just right, a trail of rivers spirals like tinsel across the Midwest. Nothing is more dramatic than the last lights off the California coast, then the long passage across the Pacific to Sydney, the sea vast as infinity.

I'm an unabashed fan of the way that flying opens new worlds. I get a charge from leaving three feet of snow on a frigid January morning, then lunching beneath dripping Spanish moss, to the play of a fountain surrounded by flowers in Houston. I travel to capture the flavors of lilting languages, the dances and arts of other cultures—totally different yet five hours from home. I fly to see our world without the congestion of traffic, lying clean and beautiful below, wrapped in the gauzy shawl of a new creation.

If it's possible to become an even greater fan of flying, I did so after September 11, 2001. I may owe my life to airline personnel and passengers—writing, traveling, and hugging my children today because of their heroism. I'll never know for sure, but I do know that I was sleeping twenty minutes from the White House when a jet crashed into the countryside of western Pennsylvania. Had it been intended for a target in Washington?

Did Captain Jason Dahl cut the fuel line? Did a flight attendant pour boiling water on a hijacker? Did passengers who knew they were doomed divert the murderous course and save countless lives? No one will ever know the answers, but we live in the mystery of those questions, grateful for every breath, every step.

I am more thankful than ever for the buttery glow of autumn leaves along a runway, for the silhouette of a sleek bird in the sky, for the surge of energy as a jet accelerates and the grace of its fierce, proud liftoff. For centuries, humans lived confined to the small space where their feet or their horse could take them, then to a larger field where they could drive. But the gift of flight, enticingly fraught with danger and potential is unique to our age. Lindbergh and Earhart struggled to achieve what we easily assume.

For too long we've taken it for granted. With minimal fuss, we can be borne aloft to San Antonio's River Walk and Chicago's Lake Shore Drive, the Golden Gate and the Florida Keys, friends and families, warm beaches and frothy shores, ski slopes and tropical gardens, weddings and conventions, nasty and balmy weather, starry and blustery nights, foggy and crystal clear climates.

"Prepare for takeoff" has invited me to a larger world, which with glee I have also shown my children. We've stayed in a few roach motels and some quirky B & Bs, but we've also eaten fresh lobster in Boston and watched the balloons rise over the Sonoma Valley. We've had interminable waits and bothersome delays, but we've also snuggled into the rare treat of first class.

With leather seats, lemon towels, and warm chocolate chip cookies, who wants to land?

On September 15, 2001, edgy with fear, anxious to be home, I boarded a flight in Philadelphia. Along with the other passengers and crew, I paused in silence to remember our recent loss. Many of us were teary about crew members and passengers who once sat in these seats as we did, but whose safe landing was tragically aborted. When the flight landed, everyone aboard broke into genuine, spontaneous applause.

I really don't know what we were applauding: safety, home, personnel who carried on despite heavy hearts. Or maybe, subconsciously, we cheered our freedom; we hadn't been deterred by the twisted minds and brutal intentions of nineteen men. We had seen the broader picture, the larger story. We seized the vision then and will continue to soar because the great stories never end; in some form or another, they always continue. Maybe we cheered because we were still participating in the difficult, glorious, wrenching, exquisite, tedious, breathtaking world of air travel today.

Of course I've spent time in long security lines, grumbled about getting to the airport early, had my itinerary rearranged, and missed a few flights. For all I know, that once easy world of privilege has vanished. But still I want to cast my lot with the surly and gracious, crusty and compassionate, nit-picking and generous, stonewalling and efficient folks who run the airlines—people with all the same qualities of the diverse human race. I like the adrenaline rush of making a connection with four minutes to spare. I can't bear to see the adventure end. Maybe I'm stubborn: I will not easily surrender the skies.

Moviegoing

Part 1

Hey, I'm no prude—I enjoy a raunchy movie as much as the next person. But after *this* Sunday matinee, my son and I felt like fumigating our clothes and rinsing with Listerine. Not a single adult was healthy or normal, the "guru" figure was a drug dealer, and the high point—touted in reviews as the epitome of powerful symbol—was a plastic bag blowing in the wind against a background of red brick. Watching it, one character confides breathlessly to the other, "I can barely contain so much beauty."

Well maybe if you've never seen the ocean, or heard a symphony, or read Willa Cather, or walked through a prairie in spring. On what planet do these people dwell? Preoccupied with guns, dysfunctional family scenes, and unmotivated sex bordering on child pornography, they never seemed to go to the grocery store. It was a breath of fresh air to leave the theater and see ordinary folks riding their bikes under autumn foliage. "Maybe we really *do* live in a sick society," I muttered to my son.

Searching for some antidote milder than Lysol, I returned to the reading from this morning's liturgy. We had lucked out there, hearing a passage from Philippians beautifully proclaimed by a woman scripture scholar. Even later in the quiet of home, it stood inspiringly against the cesspool of the movie:

Finally, beloved, whatever is true, whatever is honorable, whatever is just, whatever is pure, whatever is pleasing, whatever is commendable, if there is any excellence and if there is anything worthy of praise, think about these things. (4:8)

On such things—beauty and compassion and wonder and love—we set our hearts. We cannot be turned aside by some slick theatrical view of life which the critics praise and which has very little relation to reality. Like Jesus whose society was also sick, we don't let human failures silence the praise which rightly belongs to God.

Part 2

A sucker for a good movie review, I hurried to the latest Japanese flick which had won four stars. The premise of *After Life* wasn't bad: a person newly deceased gets three days to select the happiest or most precious memory of their life. Then a film crew re-creates it as accurately as possible, and they carry it into the next life, to live in that moment eternally.

Some of the moments were lovely—an elderly woman whose face was a wonderful wrinkly texture chose the day in childhood when her brother bought her a red dress and she danced in it. A former soldier, hungry and weary at the end of the war, remembers smoking a cigarette and eating rice provided by American troops, thinking, "I could get along with these people!" Another woman recalls meeting her future husband on a bridge after she thought he had died in battle. Their reunion in the crowd meant her future—seventy years later, she could describe the sunlight glinting on the water beneath the bridge.

I spent the slower moments, as I'd guess much of the audience did, wondering which moment I would choose under the circumstances. I reeled back through many splendid times, but got quickly annoyed with the process. Who said I must choose only one? Why was it so arbitrary? And did I really want to spend eternity frozen in the same memory, even if it was a happy one?

Perhaps there is something to be said for the more traditional notion of heaven. To the Christian, eternal life represents far more than even our best times on earth. What we look forward to above all is seeing the face of God. Beside that vision, earthly happiness pales. The presence of those we love who have died before us will presumably be part of the joy, but heaven is ultimately the fulfillment of our hearts' deepest desires.

The Book of Revelation describes heaven as the place where God will wipe away every tear, and there will be no more mourning or pain (21:4). Of course it's hard to picture; one video cassette is much easier to wrap our imaginations around. But shouldn't the afterlife be the fulfillment of our largest hopes, our furthest-reaching yearnings, the desires we can barely articulate? Humans are made for a greater scope than we ever envision; surely heaven is the place where all longing comes to rest in one beloved face.

The two movies represented two ends of a spectrum: at one end, movies that disgust; at the other, those that delight. The medium at its best lends itself to reflection because it frames life and freezes it. Sometimes it can lead us back into reality sensitized to its possibilities, more attentive to the beauties there. Even if the movie has been only a comic escape on Friday night, we leave the darkened theater blinking, refreshed. As Beatrice Bruteau writes, "When we take a little time to remember, to look, to marvel, we find that there are sources of joy, of esthetic delight, of quiet happiness on every hand."[26]

PART FOUR

Objects as Sacramentals

Love without concrete expression may be a sham. Ask people how they know that someone loves them, and a variety of objects emerge in the answers. "He bought me ice cream on a sweltering day or coffee on a chilly one." "I smell clean laundry and think of my wife." "Every time I wear this sweater my grandmother knitted, I remember her." "He brings lilacs and it scents the whole office." "I've worn this ring for thirty-two years." "Mom makes me ants-on-a-log." If love were restricted to abstract words or emotions, it would be pallid indeed. The objects give weight and substance to the feeling.

So too God's effort to communicate a passionate and abiding love for humanity takes shape in objects. Many who have wanted to know God have thus turned to the language of sensate signs. For centuries, bread and wine, oil and water, fire and ashes have communicated more than words can say. To this list, we can add contemporary interpretations and objects, such as computers, sundaes, and Christmas ornaments.

Mary Oliver is a modern poet who reads God's language in objects. She writes, "I could not be a poet without the natural world. . . . For me the door to the woods is the door to the temple. . . . I am sensual in order to be spiritual." She explains that her day always begins with a walk outdoors. There she marvels at a blue grosbeak or a black oak. When she returns, her partner always asks, "How was it?" Oliver always answers, "It was wonderful."[1]

The original notion of the sacramental object derives from the belief that grace is mediated by nature. So the statue, the harp, or the stained glass window have long spoken to people of God. Andrew Greeley, champion of the sacramental imagination, says of these objects, "They are poor metaphors for God's love, but metaphors just the same."[2] The ancient Celts once blessed the loom, the cow, the peat fire, and the beer vat. What in contemporary life has replaced these traditional objects? For each person the answer differs, but this section contains a few suggestions.

As you read this section, be sensitive to the question:

What objects reveal God to you?

Then spend some time in reflection or discussion about objects that prompt you to think of God, praise God, or bring you closer to God.

Christ for the Confused

Aprevailing confusion about the institutional church isn't new. In some ways, believers today resemble the early Christian community. Imagine a people whose whole identity and history is Jewish. Their parents have handed on that tradition, have raised them with its customs, music, food, and poetry. When they pray, they turn to the sacred text of the Psalms or Torah. Their thought patterns, their lifestyles, their ways of worship are all Jewish. They cling to their heritage tenaciously, valuing it especially because the larger, Roman world disregards it. And now they must give it up.

This group was the audience for John's gospel. Their whole liturgical life was Jewish, yet the threat of extinction had made their religion rigidly orthodox. After the destruction of the temple in 70 A.D., Jews who believed in Jesus were cut off from the synagogue.[3] Feeling uprooted and disoriented, they wondered what in the new could ever replace the old.

The words that John addressed to them can speak to us today. We wonder what to preserve as familiar institutions crumble. While we're bored by grandma's rosary or Ladies' Missionary Society, we envy her steady joy and firm conviction. We want to jettison the irrelevant and the unjust, yet still want to pass on a core of meaning to our children. We know our tradition contains gold nuggets, yet sometimes we feel adrift like John's community, wondering where to turn.

To us John offers a vision of Jesus that is sacramental because Jesus so clearly identifies himself with physical, tactile, ordinary objects. "If you want to find God," he says, "look around. See that gate? that vine?

that loaf? All these speak of me." This vision replaces what is lost, proclaiming God's unstinting urge to bypass barriers and come to *all* people, even those who don't understand obscure theological terms. God communicates clearly because God refuses to be distanced from any of God's people.

To legalists today, John says what he said to the Pharisees of his day. The law is not a problem; it has simply been superseded in the new order (1:17). So he refers to "your" law and "your" synagogue, meaning that they concern only the Jews now, not Christians.[4] He encourages timid, bewildered followers that Jesus has replaced Jewish institutions and feasts.

In the same vein, John assures us that we already possess eternal life, that we are already God's children, and that, in short, we have everything we need.[5] If those statements seem abstract, his images invite us into the very heart of Christ. He frames Jesus' identity in concrete, easily understood metaphors that invite us to respond imaginatively. In the world of the imagination, accessible to all, bitter and exclusionary debate over doctrine becomes irrelevant. The image, like the lotus, simply unfolds silently, beautifully.

To the question "who is God?" that has puzzled thinkers for centuries, John's Jesus responds with simple, organic comparisons: bread, light, gate and shepherd, life, path and vine. Jesus' "I am" sayings carry on the revelation of God begun in the Old Testament. The particular set on which we'll focus is functional, meaning they do not define Jesus in himself but indicate who he is in relation to human beings. John shows his community how Jesus takes the place of tabernacle (gate and light), manna (bread), and religious leader (shepherd). His message to them rings true for us: when you have Jesus, you have everything you need. Even if you only seek him, you have enough, because God in turn is seeking you.

Bread of Life (Jn 6:35, 51)

A universal word for spiritual longing seems to be "hunger." Those who have known physical hunger know how gnawing and all-consuming it can become, distracting us from almost anything else at hand. To hunger spiritually is much the same: life's usual attractions lose their appeal if we cannot ground them in meaning, give them some significance beyond themselves. A common complaint is that churches fail to feed this hunger. In the words of Scottish poet Robert Burns' mother, seeing his monument in Edinburgh after he died of starvation: "You asked for bread and they've given you stone."

To such deep hunger, Jesus responds. From the very beginning of his life, he came to nurture us. A telling detail is repeated in Luke's infancy narrative. Mary lays her son in a manger (2:7) and the shepherds find him lying in the manger (2:16). Because a manger is a trough where animals feed, the symbolism is clear: Jesus is food. Born in the town called Bethlehem ("house of bread"), he gives the sustenance without which we die.

In the Old Testament, the coming of the messiah was often portrayed as an intimate banquet with God (see Prv 9:5; Is 55:1-2). Jesus announces that the banquet has arrived and invites us to eat. But he introduces a new twist, identifying himself as the bread that gives life. Scripture scholar Raymond Brown points out, "Under all these metaphors of bread, water and life, Jesus is symbolically referring to the same reality, a reality which, when once possessed, makes a man see natural hunger, thirst, and death as insignificant."[6]

For a Jewish audience, he replaces with his own body the manna given in the desert (6:32). For us, his theme echoes in the words of consecration at the eucharist: "this is my body which is given *for* you; this is my blood, which will be poured out *for* you." It is a sad irony that the eucharist, intended as a source of unity and nurture, should be twisted into a debate over who can come to the table. A truly sacramental outlook can transcend the divisions of thought and the eligibility requirements. It sees that if one piece of bread can become holy, all bread should be reverenced. One day just after communion, a man who'd struggled with doubt realized, "This is all I will ever need. This faith. This God. This Jesus."[7]

Light of theWorld (Jn 8:12; 9:5)

In a murky world, all we ask is a little light. Ask anyone who's endured a stretch of gray weather (either internal or external) what difference it makes when sun cascades on the scene. Sometimes we need light within, to focus on our blind spots. Sometimes we need it without, to clarify obscure situations. So we turn to the Christ who came as light, who tried to illuminate any darkness that separated people from God. Repeatedly, he tried to attune them to their own inner light, that spark of divinity that fires every human being.

On dark corners of his world, he shone fully, without restraint. Jesus' words, "I am the light of the world. Whoever follows me will never walk in darkness but will have the light of life" are not empty: immediately after this announcement, he cures the man born blind. His healing action infuriates the religious authorities, who threaten to excommunicate him and his parents. The miracle that should be applauded and celebrated becomes instead the grounds for vilification and argument. How frustratingly human: to glimpse the divine radiance, then turn back to the dark comfort of grinding discord.

Gate (Jn 10:7-10) and Shepherd (Jn 10:11, 14)

To people like the blind man in chapter nine who rejected the Pharisees' unjust exercise of authority, Jesus offers himself as a leader who will better serve the people. The Old Testament contains the raw material for Jesus' "creative reinterpretation."[8] In Ezechiel 34,

God condemns the shepherds who fatten themselves but neglect the sheep. "I myself will seek them out," God promises those scattered over the mountains, left as food for wild animals.

We who have grown weary of self-serving leaders and deceptive governments must resist cynicism when we hear such a promise. Yet Jesus gives the ultimate weight to his words, finally giving his own life for ours. To those overwhelmed by choice and puzzled by alternatives, he offers himself as the one gate, the true direction. Interestingly, neither metaphor robs the individual of free choice. The shepherd acts only as guide; the gate merely gets us where we're going. The final decisions are still up to us.

We need to examine whether we have become imprisoned in ingrained habits of thought, elevating custom into doctrine. But if Jesus is our gate and way, we can think more creatively and act more confidently. We can resist external attempts to lord it over us or inner apathies that surrender the work of thinking to someone else. Gradually, we learn to take seriously Paul's words, "If God is for us, who is against us?" (Rom 8:31).

Resurrection and Life (Jn 11:25)

Pieties are an insult to those whose grief is bottomless. Christ's promise is especially addressed to those who mourn. "I will be for you even beyond the walls of this world and the limits of this life. Even into eternity I am for you." His words come as salve to the sorest ache, ointment for the worst wound. If there *is* any answer to death, any adequate resistance to the great thief, Jesus holds the most hope because he follows word with action.

Not only does he promise Martha that her brother Lazarus will see some distant resurrection in the next life, he brings him back to *this* life, here and now. He uses the present tense because his resurrection is not only the hope of some foggy future. In every day are "small r" resurrections just as there are "small s" sacraments. After a tiring day, we go to bed exhausted, befuddled, unable to think clearly or make decisions. But after restorative sleep, we wake ready and able for a new day. At eighty-three, a man wins a marathon; at fifty-five, a woman starts her Ph.D.; at forty-five, a mother works on her GED.

In all of human history, Jesus has been the only one who can burst open the tomb. His resuscitation extends beyond physical death to other areas of psychic death: the stale relationship, the career that has lost its zing, the places in our lives that grow mold. To these as well, he brings the resurgence of energy, the health after illness, the rekindling of interest which we thought had long gone.

Way, Truth, and Life (Jn 14:6)

Sometimes, befuddled by decisions, we just want someone else to tell us what to do. "Point me in the right direction," we ask half-seriously. When Jesus offers himself as the path, he answers our frustrations with aimless wandering and incoherence.

However, this path is not cost-free. One huge risk is assuming that "with Jesus at my side, I can do no wrong." Ego can easily masquerade as discipleship. So the path requires time given to thought in solitude, serious conversation with intimate friends, committed reading, and learning. Good resources abound, well worth the time to search. Few people would embark on a career without constant updating and inservicing. Yet how many pay equal attention to their ultimate direction and final destination? To this path we must bring our best selves: head, heart, hands, and feet.

Vine and Branches (Jn 15:1, 5)

Anyone who has visited a tropical climate has seen how vines can grow with wild abandon. Control is useless; green leaves cascade over trees, strangle clear-ings, and threaten gardens. The kudzu or ivy exudes a profusion of life: expanding, creeping, growing every-where. John invites us to imagine life with Jesus like that. Just as it is impossible to picture a vine and its branches separately, so his life and ours are integral parts of each other. It is a vibrant metaphor, like the lung and the air that fills it, or the wine that must taste of its own grapes.

Again, Jesus puts a new slant on "raw material" from the Old Testament. In Hosea, Isaiah, and Jeremiah, the vineyard was often a symbol for Israel, spanning both its fruitfulness and its desolation. Now Jesus applies to himself this term used for Israel. None of the Old Testament passages stresses the vine as the source of life for the branches as Jesus does.[9] Again, God is for us in a way that is as lavish and life-giving as ivy.

By defining himself through objects and people, Jesus speaks clearly and directly. He avoids protracted debates about dogma, preferring instead to prompt the imaginative processes. He makes himself accessible to all, not just those with doctorates in theology or train-ing in rabbinical school. His images aren't hard and fast, but a country without borders, which we can end-lessly explore.[10]

Water and Oil:
Baptism and Confirmation

Trying to follow Christ is not a one-time event but a continuous process. So while baptism marks our welcome into the Christian community, subsequent experiences with water deepen our relationship with God and echo that first immersion. Water in different forms renews the ongoing gifts of baptism: beauty, identity, light, healing, potential, community, and eternal life.

Snorkeling: Beauty

Getting the hang of snorkeling is a matter of resting one's forehead on the sea, stroking one's fins, listening to the steady sound of one's breathing, and discovering a whole new world. How few people ever see the mountain ranges and Grand Canyons beneath the ocean—yet how much care the Creator poured into them.

On a coral reef grow canyons and cathedrals, plates and cauliflowers, branching forests in purple and pink. Dazzling tropical fish carry on their sides whole mosaics, shimmering gold and green. Tiny iridescent blue fish interweave with silvery black and white ones, giant tortoises and rays. No one choreographs the ballet, but all move with fluttering tranquility. The person lucky enough to peer into this remarkable vista leaves with deep peace and joy, a witness to one of the world's wonders.

Surely one reason we are drawn to water is its mysterious beauty. We become absorbed in the shifting patterns of light, changes in depth, a multicolored surface—here opal, there jade, now gray-blue. Beauty is

God's beacon, opening the door to hope. It heralds the best in this life and a time to come when all will be beautiful.

Walking along a shore glazed by water, it is sometimes hard to tell where ocean stops and land begins. So, too, when the delicate watercolors of pastel skies blend with the horizon, it is hard to distinguish ocean from sky. In the presence of great beauty, our sublime happiness may spring from the fact that we are precariously poised on a similar boundary—between this world and the next.

Beauty comes as a message from God, drawing us back to God. And we are caught happily in the loop.

Mountain Stream: Identity

After the water bath of baptism, we are not left shivering and defenseless. We are given a white garment to represent our new identity, clothed in Christ. At the funeral, the pall drapes the casket to recall the baptismal garment. And our identity as God's daughter or son remains the constant throughout a life where personal and professional identities can change frequently. Many women go from daughter to wife to mother to grandmother to widow. Throughout a career, we may change roles several times. A recently retired dentist delighted in the transition he'd made from using his instruments on teeth to discovering a variety of other uses. "They make great paint brushes for the tiniest spots!" he gloated. "And the little mirror helps me find things I drop when I'm fixing my car!"

I recently took a class in the mountains, troubled by my new identity as a retreat director. I had signed up for the class on retreat design full of questions and anxieties. The frenzy of activity around the hummingbird feeder at the site captured my inner state. I wasn't confronting major problems, but issues that in retrospect were only hummingbird wars. Compared to my state of mind, the whirring wings looked still. I buzzed internally around questions of whether to give retreats, how to give retreats, how to resolve practical difficulties.

The anxieties poured out during one intense conversation with the teacher. She handled them graciously, and almost as an afterthought commented, "But we must believe this is God's work, not ours." I floated down the stairs from her office and found a bench by a nearby creek where I could think about her words. They were, I discovered, the perfect advice.

St. Paul's words finally made sense: "it is not I who live, but Christ lives in me." All minor difficulties washed away in light of this revelation. If God was working in me, couldn't that power overcome my fears? If God was the force and I was simply the channel, then leading retreats wasn't about ego or perfection or performance. The insight freed me to lay down a huge burden of needless worry.

The stream beside me ran like an undercurrent to my thoughts. I reflected there on the only song that could capture so much joy and praise: Mary's "Magnificat." "For the Mighty One has done great things for me" (Lk 1:49). Her words sang soprano against the alto background of the brook splashing stones.

A friend had told me recently how her three-year-old son takes on the Batman persona when he wears the cape and mask. So I wore imaginatively the baptismal gown of an infant. "Put on Christ" writes Paul. If we don Jesus' identity, respecting it above all others, grace rushes into our lives like a stream, cascades like a waterfall.

A Walk After Rain: Light

When we are worn down by the same tired routines, habituated to repeated patterns, we need grace like a spray in the face, the cold shower of surprise. It came for me one morning after rain. I never realized how the play of light enhances water. But that morning, branches were sequined and shrubbery became a net for the light. Tiny green leaves cupped jewels of water, held light like pearls.

The landscape glimmered and shone, like a familiar scene suddenly festooned with tiny white Christmas lights. I walked like a child in a fairy tale, through a magical landscape, trying to look everywhere at once. As soon as the day warmed, the water would evaporate and the effect would vanish. But for a little while, I was all eyes.

That experience may have been a reminder of who we really are. Scripture repeatedly tells of our royal lineage, but we never quite understand until that identity is made concrete. Diadems tangled in the grass, necklaces looped the bushes. And if God so clothes the lilies, how much more so we who are dim in seeing and slow in catching on.

In the baptismal rite, we are handed a candle and called to bear the light of Christ. In the Easter Vigil, the candle dances in the water. That morning the two symbols came together: light and water, and I was bejeweled by both.

Pacific Beach: Healing

In the ancient world and today, oil symbolizes healing and strengthening. In an arid climate, the film of sunscreen protects; ointment soothes a wound; and after a bath, lotion makes the skin supple and fragrant. That combination of oil following water has always represented cleansing and cure. The post-baptismal anointing is echoed by an anointing with chrism in the sacrament of confirmation.

I hadn't thought much about the healing properties of the baptismal symbols until three days on the Pacific coast gave me ample time to walk beside that vast body of water. The rhythm of waves led to reflection on two verses from Psalm 51:

Wash me thoroughly from my iniquity,
and cleanse me from my sin. . . .
wash me, and I shall be whiter than snow. (51:2, 7)

Contemporary people need to be washed not only from guilt and sin, the heavy burdens of the past, but also from the anxieties that creep into each day, the stresses that bear down on the shoulders, the tensions that tighten the neck muscles. We are plagued by worries we can do little about so we internalize them. Our prayer becomes the plea of the Catholic Mass, "deliver us from all useless anxieties."

Responsible sorts have a hard time knowing the difference between situations we can control and those we can do nothing about. The sea restores perspective to our dilemmas, hinting in its vastness at the grandeur of God. It reminds us that in God's providence, our nagging cares are swept away by the wind and drowned in the crash of waves. Then ocean waters make tangible the healing touch of the divine.

Morning: Potential

I try to read about the perichoresis of the Trinity, a concept I really like for its image of God dancing, all three partners circling together. But I cannot concentrate when a songbird symphony is striking up outside the window. What is the energetic dance if not translated into the delights of every day? The down comforter which covers me like a cloud of warm air, newly planted window boxes and just-mown lawn, the smell of water from the hose on the grass, the energizing crispness of morning air, the plans for the day, the high expectations of activities that will fill it. Of course there is too much to do, like any other good day. By the end, I will tire and regret all that has not been accomplished.

But for this moment now, all is fresh potential. A sense of new beginnings can bless each day, bathe it in wonder and creativity. Philosopher Beatrice Bruteau characterizes baptism as "God promises us and promises in us." "God, by baptizing you, promises you that fresh Beginning over and over again. . . . Feel the confidence of that, the power of it, the joy of it."[11] A new baby is one of the clearest signs we humans have for a new beginning. But a new baby doesn't come along every day, so we look instead to the early hours of morning as a reminder that anything is possible, that newness can mark even the oldest project or the most exhausted and broken person.

Hot Tub: Community Remembered

Few pleasures compare with ending a cold day in a hot tub. While the waters soothe the muscles, the soul relaxes too. It is hard to take oneself too seriously as the limbs turn to jelly and the body floats like dead weight. It must be impossible to do calculus in a hot tub.

What is quite possible, I've found repeatedly, is to review the day's events in a detached and dozy way. What once mattered so intensely loses its edge; Big Trouble becomes mere irritation. While some might argue that a few drinks would have the same effect, scientists have not yet discovered health risks in hot tubs. (Or if they have, they're too relaxed to tell.)

The physical experience is delicious enough, but sometimes I add a mental litany of friends. I revisit those who phoned or e-mailed that day, cozy arrangements for lunch or travel, plans still full of potential. My instinctive thought pattern is reinforced by a sacramental theologian who writes: "If one looks at baptism theologically, one can see that 'entry into the Christian community' has an intrinsic primacy among the significances of the ritual. After all, it is by being introduced into the believing community that one comes to Christian faith."[12]

Celtic peoples had an ancient custom of birth-baptism which immediately followed birth and preceded the clerical baptism in church eight days later. After each tiny drop of water placed on the small forehead, the watching-women would say "Amen." One commentator writes of this "small s" sacrament: "Ear has never heard music more beautiful than the music of the watching-women when they are consecrating the seed of man and committing him to the great God of life."[13]

Sometimes, outdoors, I am bathed not only in water but also in the light of the full moon. Add to that the warm memory of friends and it's as perfect an experience as humans are likely to get this side of paradise. So water speaks to us of God: warming us, relaxing us, restoring community.

Fountain: Eternal Life

When I work at home, a small, desktop fountain provides a trickling undertone to my work. One of the most soothing sounds to the psyche is running water, and this provides a quiet music even when I am pounding away at a keyboard or stuck in an awkward sentence construction. While it doesn't carry conscious associations of baptism, perhaps they linger subconsciously.

Or maybe the flowing sound reminds me of days on boats or picnics by streams. For those who don't have the comforting lap of wave outside the window, it's the next best thing. When the flow of words or ideas stalls, the water of the fountain continues to fall like rain or drop like little bells. Somehow it connects me to a natural world where waterfalls cascade and rivers rush to the sea.

Some fascination with fountains must encourage city planners to put them in public places and architects to include them in their designs. In the midst of traffic, pollution and congestion, their pure plash recalls the shore, the lake, or the river. People rest or eat beside them and souls are nourished as well as bodies. Pleading for crystalline cascades in every plaza, essayist J. B. Priestley calls them "fountains like wine, like blue and green fire, fountains like diamonds—and rainbows in every square."

Beneath a canopy of oaks draped with Spanish moss, a fountain bubbles before a southern mansion. Mossy stone cherubs hold it up and the sheets of water sing a gracious abundance. Birds gather as do people, drawn to this life source, this lavish flow. In a tiled southwestern courtyard, the fountain is circled with flowers like a garland. The tiny yellow cups fill with reflected light and drops of water, as if the two lend each other life.

Ultimately, fountains tell us something about human life mingled with the divine: joyous, overflowing, free. The richness of God's life is "the interior fountain that never fails."[14] In the unending cycle of waters spirals an image for lively grace, sparkling in the sun.

Jesus offered the woman at the well "a spring of water gushing up to eternal life" (Jn 4:14). The fountain within her must have danced when he overlooked her past, her ethnicity, and placed himself on her level, the level of basic need. The inner fountain must have leaped again when he made no judgment on the long litany of husbands who failed. Hope leaped again when he mentioned that worship was confined neither to Gerizim nor Jerusalem, but flourished within the human temple.

Thirsty Hebrews once asked the ultimate question, "Is the Lord among us or not?" (Ex 17:7). If we've never asked that question, we simply do not understand the struggle. In answer, Jesus stands beside all the wells of our lives, saying, "Reach deeper. Go further. Find me. The answer is yes."

Aftereffects

We cannot spend a day without water; try it and seriously endanger health. Perhaps because of this dailiness, this constancy, it can remind us frequently of our identity in Christ. Just as his baptism celebrated who he was, so we cannot hear often enough the words addressed to him: "You are my beloved child. In you I am well pleased." Applying that affirmation to ourselves strengthens who we are at the profoundest level.

Joyce Rupp imagines what it was like for Jesus, hearing those words for the first time:

> *He must have felt a surge of tenderness wash over him. A strong, assuring conviction of his relationship with God must have become firmly stored in his soul at that time. Jesus felt this power again and again in his life as he came forth from the desert, as he healed the sick, as he spent the nights alone in prayer, as he stood up for his beliefs, as he communed with his friends, as he walked the road to Calvary.*[15]

We too feel the effects of our baptisms, just as we taste water on a parched tongue or soothe lotion on sunburn. Perhaps it comes when we solve a dilemma or make a stand for justice. Maybe we feel that tenderness when we look at those we hold dear. In an ordinary day, we experience a fountain of laughter, a drop of balm, a shower of beauty, a deep pool of compassion, a stream of energy. Through water and oil we are connected with all that is most true and beautiful about ourselves.

The word "baptism" means to plunge into. While the hot tub might be a cozy image, the sacraments call us always beyond affirmation and celebration to the tough arenas of the world. We are anointed not simply to feel the silkiness of oil on the skin but to be strengthened for service. The early Christians knew that a savage Roman world would not welcome them gladly. So they bathed and anointed like soldiers going into battle or athletes preparing to compete. We follow the same sequence: plunge in, drink deep, oil, go forth to serve.

Candle Fire

If the candle graces an altar, can it not have the same effect on a desk or dining table? It reminds us of one whose coming was heralded by a star, who dispelled darkness saying, "I am the light of the world" (Jn 8:12). The perfect oval of candle flame lights vigils after horrendous violence plunges the survivors into the shadows. Despite brutal deaths, the candles appear, giving substance to the promise of Isaiah:

> *See, darkness covers the earth,*
> *and thick clouds cover the peoples;*
> *But upon you the Lord shines,*
> *and over you appears God's glory.*
> *Nations shall walk by your light,*
> *and kings by your shining radiance. (60:2-3, NAB)*

Moving now from the more dramatic setting to the more usual, here are two instances of candles. The reader, of course, will add more.

Candles on the Desk

Most people have rituals for going to work, as I do twice a week when I go to my office downtown. The process includes the bath, the dress, the briefcase that must contain relevant papers, books, correspondence, and schedules. Even weekend travel to give a workshop or retreat begins in ritual: packing, driving to the airport, parking in the same area, checking in, visiting the airport perfume shop for a sample squirt.

But working at home begins with an entirely different ritual. Clothing is no longer so important; sweats will do fine. What *is* important is a ritual that sets the tone for a day of writing. On my desk are three candles, each with special memories. One, given to me long ago at a workshop site, promised thirty-two hours of burning, and is holding to the promise. Another came from a closing retreat ritual, where the minister invited us to take our candles home and light them when we felt alone. A third, shaped like a gift box, concretizes a friend's belief that we are gifts to each other.

While none of these associations seems profound, the simple act of lighting the candles says something significant, as it has in many religions. It implies that what we do is holy and important. Candlelight graces the most ordinary dinner and dignifies the simplest dwelling. Perhaps it suggests an older era, re-creates romantic notions of people living with more graciousness, space, and slow time than we have. We endure voice mail, the threat of violence, and incompetent service on a regular basis—perhaps we light the candle to offset the daily indignity, to restore some distant, dimly imagined birthright.

We also light a candle for its spiritual significance. A candle suggests dedication and ritual; where it glows, space is sacred and the hours it lights are holy. A friend lit one every time she struggled with grueling paperwork proving how lawyers had taken advantage of her family during a painful divorce. She wanted her children to know she was doing arduous but important work to protect them.

As I write, a candle on the desk reminds me that this is a holy task. It stands as mute prayer that my words might help someone. Its flame unfolds beautifully as a trillium. It rests in a glass holder on a mirror base that came with a card reading: "All beauty mirrors the divine beauty, all holiness on earth is the fragrance of God present with us, and at the core of all creation flames the creating love of God."

The drafts may look messy and disorganized now, but some day, bound and printed, the book may touch people's lives. In some way I can't imagine now, someone will thank me. She will say, "I read a chapter of your book on the bus going to work." I'll hope I've given her a glimpse beyond asphalt to a million dew drops tangled in lush grass. Or he'll say, "You started me thinking. . . . " Then I see that look in a reader's eyes that makes long, frustrating hours alone at the computer worthwhile.

Candles on the Dining Table

The saving grace of the candle also surfaces in other settings. One is a boring dinner honoring a dear friend. The people are strangers, the speeches meander, and somehow I wind up seated beside a woman who seethes with hostility. But in the center of the table burns a candle. I focus on it during the third stale joke and mentally it takes me elsewhere, restores my firm foundation. The pure cone of light, wavering but true, stabilizes and renews.

Gazing on it, I return to that morning's prayer and work, so closely intertwined it is hard to distinguish the two. "No one can injure you," said the meditation I read then. "Nothing you could ever do could win— or lose—the love of God." In light of that, interminable dinners and stultifying boredom seem minor irritations.

What could be more important than such a reminder? The speeches drone on, but I am imaginatively lost in candle flame. Playful and golden, it sparks a dull evening and enlivens a time I thought was lost. Not a bad message, that, for such a small object. . . .

Sacramental Bonfire

Candles also open windows on a long tradition, a deeper meaning. This tiny flicker contained on desk or dining table reminds us of the dramatic sacramental use of flame during the Easter Vigil. We gather in a chilly evening around the bonfire, bless it, then carry our candles lit from it throughout a darkened church. All the while we proclaim, "Light of Christ."

We continue to evoke the symbol as we light the Easter candle, plunge it into the baptismal waters, and after every baptism, light small tapers from it. These starry pinpricks in gloom remind us of our high calling: bearers of light who can ask with the disciples on the way to Emmaus, "Were not our hearts burning within us while he was talking to us on the road?" (Lk 24:32).

While we talk about a symbol encompassing polarities, we never realize how vast those are until the safely contained fire of the Easter candle becomes an unstoppable forest fire consuming acres of land and hundreds of homes. It is then we realize more clearly what Aidan Kavanagh meant by saying, "symbols coax one into a swamp of meaning and require one to frolic in it."[16]

My own reflection on fire came shortly after huge conflagrations raged through the mountains of Colorado. Delivering my daughter to camp necessitated driving through the devastated landscape. In the surreal jumping pattern common to fires, some areas remained green and intact, while adjacent ones were nothing but stark black silhouettes of trees. The charred earth would sometimes reach right to the porch of a mountain cabin and stop. At other times, nothing was left of a home but gravel.

If St. Bonaventure was right that "every creature is a word of God,"[17] then this was difficult calligraphy. How does one interpret such devastation in sacramental terms? It reminded me of a stunned and awkward moment that sometimes occurs during the Catholic Mass. We have just heard an Old Testament tale of greed, corruption, adultery, or murder. At the lector's prompt, "The word of the Lord," we are supposed to respond, "Thanks be to God." Some folks recover quickly enough to chime in; others are still dazed by the mayhem and brutality. But I guess this odd juxtaposition frees us from accusations that God's word is sentimental or soupy. Sometimes, as in a few slaughters from the Book of Kings, it's downright bloody.

To those who lost everything in the fire, such a symbol must be utterly puzzling. Anyone who tried to place such devastation in a positive light might well be labeled Pollyanna. Yet the grace notes inevitably creep into this strange dark symphony. Generous donors wrote large checks, trying to offset loss, and less wealthy but no less thoughtful people taped their own *Grateful Dead* music for a neighbor whose collection burned. Two particular memories surface in this ambiguous, symbolic language of fire.

Gratitude

Along the main road into an area which still smoldered were posted some of the most heartfelt thank-yous I've ever read. These didn't follow the form we learned in school: painstakingly written in inky best handwriting on lined paper. In some outrageous cases, teachers made us *iron* the paper, but they couldn't force the sentiment. "Thank you for the Christmas gift," the note would begin, and drone on about a dreadful sweater until the requisite amount of space was filled.

These were different. Hand-lettered on cardboard, painted crookedly on wood or tablecloth, they proclaimed, "Thank you, firefighters for saving our home" or "God bless the firefighters. Good save!" Having seen how close the singe came in many cases, it was easy to understand this heartfelt appreciation. More organized activity followed later in thank-you concerts and potluck dinners, but there was something fresh and endearing about the tacky signs.

Grace

One attack on the fires came from the air. Helicopters filled buckets of water from nearby streams and ponds, then dumped either the water or a fire retardant on the flames. While the buckets contain eighty gallons, they looked like dangling thimbles from a distance. Beneath the tiny cup roiled an inferno pouring smoke hundreds of miles into the sky.

With high winds and intense heat, such efforts did little to slow the destruction. Concerns were increasingly grave until one day it rained. A cool, wet weekend followed, accomplishing what thousands of buckets of water and slurry had failed to do in many days. Newspaper headlines on Monday proclaimed: "Fire 80% Contained!"

The whole progression had played out St. Teresa of Avila's metaphor for the spiritual life. She describes the process of arduously dragging buckets to water a garden—then suddenly it rains. Grace accomplishes instantly what years of human effort cannot attain. Over the next several years, in the clearing made by fire, new growth will spring up. Wildflowers and greenery will cover the charred black earth.

That surge of life can be compared to our own lives. We drag through a project with little energy, then a new participant or a new angle brings a sudden vitality. We feel hopeless about a relationship, then it takes a dramatic turn for the better. Some neglected area of the personality stirs and awakens, and the whole person feels renewed. Even a change of season or a new terrain can give a fresh perspective. In more extreme cases, a severe depression lifts or a critical illness is cured.

Whether we describe such turnarounds in religious language matters less than whether we appreciate the disparity between the tiny bucket and the great outpouring. No matter how much we try or how hard we work, our efforts are always limited, human, small-scale compared to the pivotal gift of grace. That gift can come only from outside ourselves.

So fire gives us a small window into God's mysterious ways. A force that has both helped and plagued humanity symbolizes the Creator: warmth and light combined with terrible destruction. The symbol shows us how all our ideas of God are inadequate. It seems too easy to say that in the divine plan, devastation is not the final answer, or that the place of destruction can become the place of grace. But perhaps we can say that fire gives us a glimpse of a God who is powerful and vast beyond all imagining.

Wine: Eucharist

If wine used for consecration and communion is holy, cannot all wine be seen as potentially sacred? Again, the marvelous multiplicity of the symbol leads us to examine its many facets in experience and in scripture. As always, we are aware that the symbol encompasses polarities: its dimensions can be both positive and negative.

Mother's Day

The children surprise me by becoming chefs. With fine flourish and secretive bustle, they produce a spectacular dinner which we eat on the patio—the first time this year that it's warm enough to eat outdoors. The just-mown lawn is fragrant; the first flowers bloom in the tentative spring. In that setting, we create a circle of family at its best: we joke and poke and eat and praise the fine cuisine. Later tonight, we will scatter to jobs, other demands, and the less idyllic clean-up, but for now, we linger around the table. It is one of those moments frozen in time that parents fondly hope will live on in their children's memories.

A crowning touch makes the event more special. Just as we sit down, my oldest son brings to the table a bottle of pale pink wine. This is no ordinary wine, hastily purchased at the discount liquor store. Instead, it brings back a story; every sip carries us further into memory.

It was our first trip to the Sonoma Valley in early spring. We had driven through hills covered with blooming golden mustard, stopping at various wineries and sampling their vintages. Finally we arrived at one which, even in California's Garden of Eden, surpassed the others for picturesqueness. The driveway led beneath flowering pink trees to a wooden structure beside a water wheel. The music of turning waters filled the tasting room as we sampled. Our favorite was a wine the same pastel shade as the blossoms; without going into pretentious vinter's lingo, it tasted of strawberries and spring. In a burst of spending rare for him, my son ordered a case.

In the year that followed, the pastel wine became his gift to hosts and hostesses or a birthday tribute to a special friend. He liked taking it to a dinner because it came with a story, "The Day We Toured Sonoma Valley." Now he offered the last bottle to complete the Mother's Day feast. As we drank, we returned to the wine country in early spring with the splash of a turning water wheel.

Birthday

It will be my contribution to the birthday dinner: a bottle of wine called "Whitewater." The name, of course, unlocks the narrative. We were driving from Taos to Santa Fe along the Rio Grande. For someone like me who grew up alongside the mighty Mississippi, this trickle seemed unimpressive—surely no steamboat whistled across its waters.

Yet it had its own beauty: in the southwestern desert where water is scarce, the river created a green oasis along its banks. Higher up the canyon walls, vegetation bristled sparsely, but near the water trees were green and lush. In the history of New Mexico, the Rio Grande has meant fertility, beauty, and recreation.

Throughout this dry and somewhat unlikely setting are scattered a few wineries. We stopped at one small and unpretentious place to break a long, hot drive. This tiny outpost was a far cry from the vast California wineries. But the dusty setting didn't stop my older children from applying the wine-tasting tactics they had learned in a tour of Bordeaux. They swilled and sniffed bouquets like veterans, camouflaging what neo-phytes they really were.

The wine was so tasty, we bought bottles of Coyote and Antelope for the novelty of the names, and one of Whitewater to recall the kayakers and rafters on the Rio Grande below. As we sip it on the birthday, we will drift mentally back to New Mexico. Memories will bubble in the wine glasses, recalling Thomas Moore's insight that "Memory is a kind of poetry. It focuses our attention on the imagination of events rather than on events taken literally."[18]

Retreat

By the time I reach the retreat house for my annual week there, I feel like the walking wounded. A year is too long to be away from this place which is a spiritual home, this staff which has welcomed and mentored me for years. As anyone knows who has tried to get away from home or office for even a brief time, it takes enormous effort to "clear the decks." The accumulated detail must be dealt with before departure, and we become whirlwinds of activity to accomplish in several days what would ordinarily take weeks.

But with the help of sympathetic family and friends, the moment finally comes: whether it's all done or not, I drive into the foothills where the retreat house nestles. Because this pattern has been repeated so often, I know that I will arrive exhausted but will experience a turning point: a rich surge of energy that carries me spiritually into the following year.

However, that jumps ahead of the sequence. At Mass the first evening, I feel brain-dead. Since all I can think of is crashing into bed, my focus on the ritual is less than complete. Only two moments capture my attention. One comes as the priest holds the chalice up and begins the words of consecration: "Jesus said to his disciples, 'Take and drink.'"

Between his upraised arms, I glimpse the faces that surround him and the message is clear. He does not speak of disciples two thousand years ago. This chalice is given now to us to drink. To people who look as worn and dispirited as I do comes the wine of mystery and memory, the promise of hope.

The second attention-getter comes as I approach an old friend to drink from the cup she holds. She is saintly and serene; her wrinkles attest to long experience of nurturing faith in herself and others. She has heard many tragic stories; she has empathized with much pain; she has wept with those to whom she gives spiritual direction. From the sadness she has known comes a unique graciousness, a reverence rarely encountered. She looks tired too as she offers me the cup and says, "the blood of Christ, dear."

In more enlightened Catholic circles, it is common to call a person by the first name when offering them communion. Strangers sometimes thank me for using this personal touch as a eucharistic minister, when in fact I was cheating and reading a nametag quickly. But we should be intimately named when we approach the symbol of that covenant which is the truest meaning of our lives.

So I would not have been surprised if she called me Kathy. What touched me was her calling me "dear" instead. It seemed to say: "I know you're fatigued, and that you can barely concentrate. We have much to talk about. But for now all I can use is this term of endearment. All I can offer you is this cup—and it is everything."

The rest of the week became a sustained meditation on the meaning of wine. Before I explore some of those implications, I should assure the reader that I deplore the misuse of alcohol. I am an ardent admirer of Mothers Against Drunk Driving, and grieve for families tragically affected by alcoholism. So I refer here to a healthy, restrained use of a beverage given us by a gracious God, an ancient symbol in several religious traditions. The fact that wine can be abused does not rule out its sacred symbolism any more than does the fact that water can drown as well as cleanse, or fire can destroy as well as bring light and warmth.

A Dialogue on Cana

When my retreat director asked me to dialogue with Jesus at Cana, I began by complaining. I was here to escape work, not to fill stone water jars and drag them around! I was also annoyed at the dimness of men—Jesus included—who consistently missed the obvious. "Not a clue what your mother is trying to tell you!" I berated him in the tone I would use with a dopey child. (Remember: I was tired and cranky. Even great grace starts with reluctant nature.)

But once we got over that hurdle, the conversation was off on a roll. At first, I was caught on necessity and practicality: "If you don't fill the water jars, kid, the party's over." But earthiness is an endearing part of this story. You gotta love the wine steward who asks, "Why waste the good stuff on the drunks?" Calculating areas in my life where the wine had run dry was depressing, but a necessary prelude. After that survey, images began to coalesce and open with new meaning.

Through myth, I connected with generations who have drunk from the same cup. In the legend of the Fisher King, the King who holds the secret of the Holy Grail (revered as Jesus' cup at the last supper) is paralyzed. Furthermore, his illness affects the land: springs evaporate, trees produce no fruit, and animals stop breeding. No remedy helps until Parsival arrives and asks, "Where is the Grail?"

Avoiding that central question leads to disaster. Asking it arouses the Fisher King and the land. Mircea Eliade interprets the symbol of the Grail to mean, "Where is the supreme reality, the sacred . . . the source of immortality?" A civilization indifferent to that question perishes.[19]

Another insight came from Mechthild of Magdeburg, a favorite author and thirteenth-century mystic who told her soul, "You taste like a grape." A commentator explained that the soul *is* like a grape, with an envelope of skin that both protects it from and presents it to the outside world. Within is "a tingling, sweet softness."[20]

St. Teresa of Avila referred to the soul's inner life as a wine cellar. There, because it is God's very life, the wine never runs out. When Jesus calls himself the vine, he makes a close and immediate tie to us: you are the branches. His life is inseparable from ours. His life within is the source of great inspiriting, the inner reservoir that bubbles up in a thousand forms of creativity and compassion.

While this energy can be seen most clearly in the accomplishments of saints and artists, it nevertheless abides in all, waiting to be tapped. At our finest moments we know that powers greater than ourselves are at play. Such a vibrant source must be credited for Beethoven composing after he went deaf or Georgia O'Keeffe painting after she lost central vision. The inner ear, the inner eye surmount the failure of the physical apparatus.

At our Mother's Day and birthday celebrations, there was more to the wine than a simple drink; it opened a vein of memory and unlocked a treasure house of story. Just as there is more kick to wine than grape juice, so too there is more to the human being than bland appearance. Befuddled humans may whine about lugging six jars to Jesus. Yet under his touch, the water colors and comes to life. In union with him, we are more than human beings; we are Christ on earth. The sacrament of communion symbolizes that inner fire as well as the infusion of God-life that nurtures it.

The invitation "take and drink" has negative as well as positive overtones. The cup we may take casually represents the life crushed out of Christ, his blood spilled in the dust. Paul criticized the Corinthians eating and drinking as if the Eucharist had no special meaning: "one goes hungry and another becomes drunk" (1 Cor 11:21). These considerations may bring us back to the disclaimer: wine can feed the soul with flavor and passion, can melt our stiffness, buoy our spirits, and encourage our laughter. Yet at the same time it can contribute to the mangled wreckage of the car accident in which three teenagers die.

Such ambivalence intrigues anyone who takes symbol seriously. "The symbol reveals certain aspects of reality—the deepest aspects—which defy any other means of knowledge."[21] The symbol which comes before reason does not fit our usual logical categories.

Furthermore, the Cana story tells us something about God's trust in humans, mirroring the human trust in Jesus voiced by Mary. Only a woman of tremendous conviction could leave it at one line: "Do whatever he tells you." (She is also a woman who knows how to bide her time.) The story also prompts us to imagine the faces of uptight rabbis who suddenly see the waters for the ceremonial washings turning to burgundy. The face of Jesus must smile puckishly back at them, with the slightest hint of "Gotcha."

We might also wonder what kind of wildly generous God squanders an intoxicating vintage on people who are already tipsy. In a strange time warp, we are caught into the puzzle of "you have kept the good wine until now" (Jn 2:10). Presumably this eternal "now" applies to us, changing as we change, fitting different rhythms and phases of our lives. At times our experience seems thin, flat, and watery. Then if we are lucky, someone says, "the blood of Christ, dear." And God continues to fuel our inner life, the wine that never runs dry.

Celtic Spirituality and Modern Conveniences

Celtic spirituality yanks abstract forms of religion out of the sky. It gives faith a lyric grace and practical earthiness. But it has a certain "disconnect" from the twenty-first century.

We are no longer concerned with the thrums of the loom or the barnacles on the curragh. We do not churn our own butter or cut the corn with a sickle. It is hard to imagine ourselves midwifing children, weaving our own wool, or whispering into Bossy's ear: "There is the new moon, thou beloved one among cows."[22] Few people butcher their own hogs or grind wheat kernels for bread.

Some would lament the fact that we live at several removes from such direct experience. But why can't we reverence the marvelous convenience of dishwasher, fax machine, and microwave? The question is not whether modern inventions are good or bad—they are a given. Rather, how do we bring spirituality to the contemporary scene of office or home without feeling like we lug a cumbersome relic of a different era?

The beginning of an answer comes in four essential nuggets of Celtic spirituality. First, it is oriented to daily life, not abstract dogma. Esther de Waal, an expert in the field, compares the way she recited creeds and memorized catechism as a child with the ways Celtic children absorbed prayer: "My head was constantly engaged, my mind filled with information. But this did not involve the whole of myself, my five senses, my emotions and feelings, and above all my imagination."[23]

Like most of us, de Waal missed the sense of belonging to a family with a "common storehouse of memory and storytelling."[24] We might all envy the sung prayer and crooning that blessed the fabric of routine as naturally as breathing. It made God's presence immediate and accessible: before, behind, around, and above. De Waal comments on this second feature: a "sense of divine presence and protection are found elsewhere in the history of the Church, but . . . nowhere else is it found with quite the same intensity."[25]

Third, Celtic prayer was not confined to church, but was the constant refrain of busy people doing many things. It was essentially a lay spirituality, corresponding to the way most Christians live today. They worked hard, however, not to compete or excel, but to share their gifts. Their labors also marked human involvement in "the very process of creation."[26] A woman weaving did so with God's arm around her—which must have given a heathery blue-green tweed the colors of the Irish Sea.

Fourth, Celtic people were at home in themselves and rooted deeply in the earth, a quality particularly suited to our age of environmental awareness. As de Waal says, "The Celtic way of seeing the world never lets me forget my relationship with the earth. I treat the ground with reverence, but the ground also nurtures me."[27] Wendell Berry, one of the most compelling environmentalists of our century sounds a similar note of "the peace of wild things" offsetting despair.

Just as their rituals sacramentalized sowing and harvesting, banking the fire at night and stirring it in the morning, so we can sacramentalize our own routines. The acid test may be, will the same lyric grace with which Celtic peoples blessed the fire or loom fall flat when applied to the answering machine? Let's try an adaptation to three staples of modern living: the computer, the CD player, and the telephone. While others will prefer their own favorites, these three are dear to me. I want to see them as the Celts might: on two levels, as tools for careful work and as prompts to prayer.

Computers

For many professions like my own, computers have become a necessity. I can't imagine writing a book or editing a manuscript without one. Research has been immeasurably enriched and facilitated by the Internet. Like anything else, computers have their downsides, and I am the first to join the chorus of screaming when hours of work is wiped out in a failure of electrical power.

But just as we must not romanticize the grueling drudgery of pre-industrial Celtic people, so we must acknowledge the power outages, the less glamorous formatting and footnoting functions of computers as well.

Yet they contain the seeds of the sacramental (a marketing ploy untapped by any manufacturer!). When I can begin my day with simple clicks that provide food to the hungry, mammograms to the indigent, and aid to the rainforest, I am grateful that such web sites enable me to help.

The crafting of words has always delighted me; I play with their beauty and weigh their meanings as some would handle precious stones. The advent of the computer has made the writing process much easier; now we can move blocks of text and see the shape of a poem on a page in a way that might've intrigued Emily Dickinson.

When e-mail creates communication in minutes with friends around the country, the fabric of human interconnectedness grows stronger. When a procrastinator can still send birthday greetings and villagers in Ghana can order books or take online university courses, the human enterprise thrives.

While I do not understand the dynamics of cyberspace, I'm thankful for the e-mail humor that ranges from pie-in-face to sublime and the websites that encourage prayerful reflection. Medical use of computers brings hope; the exchange of research can join the human community in ways we never dreamed. Friendship and laughter, fact and meditation tumble together like mulligan stew or tossed salad or anything human, and in the variety lies blessing.

For us, booting up might correspond to the Celtic woman kindling the embers of the fire or stirring the oatmeal to start the day. Pausing to reflect on the computer's potential, being grateful for its powers, using its capabilities to serve others—can these actions not be filled with grace?

CD Players

The Celts didn't dream that God would be insulted by terms of machinery; their prayer was not polite or pious. I try to remember this as I turn to a battery-powered contraption that helps the heart sing and lifts the soul to praise. . . .

For years, the music in movies has lent importance to events. We know from the cues of the score when a walk in the park portends disaster or romance. Certain music heightens tension or emotion; other kinds create a light-hearted or tragic mood. Thanks to convenient CD players (and young people for whom music is *the* holistic experience), we can have "music wherever we go!" It can hearten our spirits, lend importance to our work, bring beauty to our mindless tasks, give oomph to our exercise.

Hiking near Vail on a rainy day, my energy began to flag. Then my daughter lent me her headset playing Enya—and I wanted to dance and sing. Whenever I direct a retreat, music is a crucial component, an entry into the right brain that leads many people to meditate. A whole range of emotion is available easily and electronically—from the melancholy of Irish ballads to calls for justice like "We Shall Overcome" that have galvanized peoples and movements.

A silver disc thinner than a blade can help us travel into memory, give us courage when we're struggling, transport us to other countries. It helps us lift our chins for the long haul, struggle accompanied by song. The sacramental nature of the CD player helps us see the underlying reality: what we do *is* important; in God's eyes, we *all* walk in beauty. We are more than drones who perform tasks; our spirits need uplifting too. Not only actors accompanied by string quartets create drama; music inspires us all to dance more lightly through our days.

Telephones

The Celts named the Trinity "the Three that seek my heart." Why couldn't God's voice travel across a telephone wire? The ringing of the phone often brings a rude interruption, a jangling intrusion, a maddening sales pitch. But it has its moments of blessing. . . .

People in emergency situations and those separated by long distances appreciate the voice on the phone, but more ordinary circumstances can prompt heartening calls. One came on a day when I was in pain, suffering "carpal tunnel syndrome of the shoulders," an ache brought on by too many robotic hours at the computer. Nothing major, just painful twitches in the neck.

But my daughter was concerned. At fourteen, she had just started high school. Her concerns usually ran along lines of wardrobe, cosmetics, football games, and friends. But she phoned in the midst of a hectic morning at school to see how I was doing. It was a touching gesture, and came in an appropriate context. That morning I had prayed the passage from John's gospel where Jesus assures his friends, "I will not leave you orphaned; I am coming to you" (Jn 14:18). Sometimes it works the other way—our children do not leave us orphaned.

Another day has all the potential for stultifying boredom. For starters, the office computer system is iffy. Then the colleague I work with most closely, whose advice I need desperately for a project in process, phones to say he won't be coming in. It is only ten o'clock and I panic that I'll never last 'til five.

Then the phone rings. The first call assures me that my son has returned safely from a trip, and is not, as I always rush to suspect, splattered across a wheat field in Kansas. The second comes from a friend I have not spoken to in months. His sense of humor always tweaks, confounds, pokes, and utterly delights. We talk for an hour, and damn the long distance bills. When I hang up after our conversation, I am smiling. Through the rest of the day, his comments filter in and out of consciousness; I revisit his humor.

A surge of energy enters my work; the best name for it is joy. The project that had stalled leaps and lumbers forward. Insights enter and research enhances. With something of the original vision recaptured, I plunge boldly and audaciously ahead. My coworker will be puzzled when he opens this bulging file tomorrow: did lightning strike?

Just as the bell once called centuries of believers to worship or contemplation, so the telephone rings. And sometimes it still brings inspiration.

A Sundae,
A Sprig of Lavender,
A Word

A butterscotch sundae that sticks to your teeth and makes your mouth ache with sweetness once became the carrier of memory.

As I licked the caramel from the spoon in an indulgence rare for the exercise-hyped and the health-conscious, it all came back. I was nine or ten again, participating in the Saturday Shopping Ritual. In the fifties, this was not a quick car trip when people wore jeans and drove to the local mall. This was Ceremony. My mother wore a dress and heels; we walked to the bus stop, then rode the bus downtown. The ritual was always the same. After visits to several department stores, we'd go to the tea room for lunch.

Sometimes we'd meet her friends there, or Grandmother, regal in her gloves and hat. I suppose we ate some real food, but all I remember was dessert. It never varied. Mine was always a butterscotch sundae created like a merry-go-round. On top was a paper umbrella, lodged in a cherry. Animal crackers marched in a circle around the little glass cup.

For an imaginative child, it represented a pinnacle of creativity. As the ladies' conversation swirled irrelevantly around me, I carefully distributed the caramel sauce to blend in equal parts with the vanilla ice cream. Then came the best part: the feet of the animal crackers, dipped soggily in the gooey sweetness. Such a dessert is not likely to appear in a gourmet magazine's virtuous "light and luscious" recipes, based mainly on fresh fruit.

The rest of the day was downhill. I didn't engage with much enthusiasm in any more shopping, and often fell asleep on the homeward-bound bus. Yet forty years later, the taste of a butterscotch sundae can restore the gracious and gentle ladies who shepherded me through department stores and always made sure we had dessert. Long dead now, they come alive for the few moments before the ice cream melts.

*

This same retrieval of memory happened for my student in a creative writing class. I had read some-where that smell was the sense most closely tied to memory. So I replicated an exercise in which students would sample various smells, then write about the memories that surfaced. (I am always grateful that some university administrator did not pass my class-room door as the students dutifully sniffed their small envelopes of various powders.) Some were stirred by the garlic; others responded to the coffee. But the strongest response came from a student who eagerly sniffed the lavender cut from my garden that morning. His ensuing essay described how he had buried his dog, the great friend of his childhood, beneath a laven-der bush. The writing was powerful, and he confessed in amazement, "I haven't thought about that in fifteen years!"

*

When a favorite uncle died recently, one of my best memories was of his enduring a long ceremony, full of boring speeches, simply for the few moments in which I received an award. Later, I worried aloud that it had been a colossal waste of time for this father of five, busi-ly engaged in an active profession. "Of course not, dar-lin'," he replied. "We were just so proud of you!"

While I knew it would be difficult to see his family after his death, I was compelled to visit them almost immediately. Somehow I knew that in their warm pres-ence my uncle would live on. So it shouldn't have sur-prised me when a tall cousin, a son who strikingly resembled his dad, swept me up in a hug and the phrase, "Hi, darlin'!" If someone had punched me in the lung, it probably would not have taken my breath away any more dramatically. In one word, "darlin'," my cousin had brought his father back to life.

Later I read that a culture creates an extensive vocabulary for whatever it most values. The Eskimos have many words for snow because they experience its many different types. And the Irish have fifty-four varieties of the word "darling." Somehow it pleases me immensely that the same word can echo out of the past into the present and a future that is still ahead.

Three objects might seem insignificant—a sundae, a sprig of lavender, a word. Mircea Eliade broadens these three to other experiences, saying that we have only "to listen to good music, to fall in love, or to pray, and [we] are out of the historical present; [we] re-enter the eternal present of love and of religion."[28]

Such simple things have the power to move us out of the moment, transcend historical time, re-create the past, and resurrect the dead. We are more, then, than our particularity; we can participate in a vast rhythm of time beyond our own. As Dostoyevski says, "even one good memory can be the means of saving us."

Christmas Ornaments

As a child, I never quite understood why the Christmas tree ornaments were so carefully stored, so gingerly unwrapped, and so reverently rewrapped in tissue paper. By the time that box came out, we were close enough to Christmas that I wanted to dispense with the preliminaries and get on with the *presents*. With a big item like that looming on the agenda, why waste time on something that was just like last year?

Now as a mom, I understand better. Those tiny, fragile items catalogue many Christmases past and much family history. In a graphic, unwritten way, they contain much of what we are, and what is best about us. They show where we've traveled, what we value, and who our friends are. To any clueless visitor, they make a statement: if this family has the slightest surplus cash, it's spent not on a car or a television, but on a trip.

The Washington State ferry floats beside the red glass chiles from New Mexico and the Boston lobster. A wreath made of shells from Florida, a lighthouse from Oregon, and a fishing boat from California show our preference for coastal regions. The animal kingdom is represented by a blue-nose dolphin and an Australian koala attired in ballet skirt and slippers.

A sensitive interpreter could read the whole family history here: the San Francisco cable car from a honeymoon thirty years ago, a "baby's first Christmas" which must be at least sixteen years old, and the little boy made by a pre-schooler, now a graduate student who tries to hide it toward the back of the tree. An embroidered mouse represents the years when I had time to make ornaments, probably because I was pregnant. "To Teacher" ornaments attest to my husband's profession for thirty years; various colleagues have contributed angels, bears, and bells.

Some of the figures could tell long stories: an angel woven from straw came from friends who worked with the Peace Corps in Peru. The Santa cleverly crafted from bread dough was the gift of an art teacher, and a less artistic but just as meaningful bear came from a son's favorite fourth-grade teacher. My cousin sent the Snoopy; "Colleen the Cross Country Skier" represented a brief phase before our daughter discovered downhill, and an elderly neighbor crocheted the snowflake.

Crystal prisms took on a new meaning when a retreat director compared them to worship. Just as a prism held to clear white light breaks it into a rainbow spectrum, so worship held up to every moment shows the colors contained in the ordinary. After the tree comes down, the prisms will hang in a south window, a reminder of a time when toddlers once danced with the rainbows cast on the floor.

Our family is not the first to venerate objects; we stand in a long Christian tradition of doing so. Barbara Bedway writes, "Blessed cloth and images of the Virgin had once brought the sacred within reach of our human hands. Who would not want to cut down that wide space between us and the infinite, and put at least a shred of the dear familiar on the abstract face of God?"[29]

People and places and experiences are all celebrated on the Christmas tree. No wonder it's a reverent ritual to unwrap and hang the ornaments every year: that's our *life* boxed in tissue paper. Every family could probably tell its own stories, trials, and adventures based on texts that hang from the tree. Only rarely do we see our history displayed at once: charming and beautiful, with boredom and argument omitted. During the holidays, crèches, wreaths, candles, and trees have more than a decorative function. They direct us to see the meaning brimming in every moment, now—before it becomes a lovely memory hung as a Christmas ornament.

Seed

Ask gardeners about seeds, and their faces soften. One mom laughs, "My four boys want to muck around in the dirt anyway. So we plant pumpkins, carrots, radishes, you name it. Then we're all dirty and happy." Another woman speaks of her twenty-nine flower beds as the place where she is happiest, and chats conversationally with God as she tends the plants.

These natural, warm connotations of seed take on new meaning in February and March, when the Napa and Sonoma Valleys of California celebrate the Mustard Festival. Initially a way to attract tourists to the wine country during the off-season, it has blossomed into a hearty festival of food, wine, art, and music called the "golden season."

The name is well deserved. Hillsides and valleys are vibrant with a gold cloud floating between dormant vines. Lacy yellow stitchery transforms what would ordinarily be the dull landscape of late winter. The wild mustard heralds the coming of spring and sparks celebration throughout the wine country.

On that purely natural level, it is a lovely event. But it takes on more meaning with the story of Father Junipero Serra. He came from Spain to California when it was a vast wilderness. Traveling north from Mexico, he scattered along his path the mustard seeds which he had brought from Spain.

Returning south the following year, Serra and his band were able to follow the "ribbon of gold" where the mustard blossomed. Along that chain he eventually established missions from San Diego to Sonoma, which would later become the state's cities. Many of "Serra's rosary" of missions remain today, adobe tributes to a person's persistent faith.

Of course Serra would've known the parable of the mustard seed found in Matthew 13:31-32. Jesus marveled that from a tiny seed could spring a bush large enough to shelter the birds and provide cool shade in the heat. "Ah," he said. "The kingdom of heaven is like that. . . ."

It's interesting that it didn't describe heaven using any of the popular stereotypes. No mention of harps, clouds, or cutesy winged creatures. Instead, he speaks of the painfully slow, silent growth of seed, or the grains of yeast in dough. The process is so gradual, we rarely see it happen. The end result catches us by surprise.

The mustard seed encourages those of us who make lists in the morning of all the annoying details we must attend to, then slog through days when we never cross one off. The seed has been held sacred for centuries, since it contains humanity's nurture and continuing. Some of the most beautiful pottery and finest baskets began as vessels to protect the small, revered seed. Farmers blessed the seed as they sowed it in spring and ritually celebrated the autumn harvest of seed for the next year's crops.

If the seed could speak, it might tell us that appearances are deceptive, that a speck no bigger than a gnat contains more than we'd ever dream. It might hearten us in our small, ungallant efforts, promising that they are part of something larger than we see. When Jesus chose the growth of mustard seed as a parable of God's reign, he pointed to process, not achievement; gradual increments, not instant results.

On the same day that my poem is published, green beans start sprouting in my garden. I don't know which event is more exciting. The words over which I'd labored lying cleanly on the page? Or the green stems unbending from seed sown ten days ago? There are many kinds of seedbed.

One day after rain, I weed the lettuce, then get the mail, not realizing I'm coated in mud. It quickly stains a letter informing me that my work will be included in an anthology of twentieth-century mystics. I chortle over the irony: a muddy mystic!

Writer Cate Terwilliger brings two strains of gardening and writing together, saying "a garden lives in a kind of perpetual poetry." There among lilacs, violas, Virginia creepers, and peonies, she finds "good and decent work, simple and beautiful productivity."[30] After two days away, she is so astonished by the growth and flowering there, she almost applauds.

A great gardener named Sido once laughed when her young daughter Colette brought home a "blessed flower" from Mary's May crowning. She asked the little girl, "D'you suppose it wasn't already blessed?"[31] Perhaps the mother thought of the seed's long process, its journey through the soil to flower—undeniable blessing.

Planting a handful of seed corresponds to the unfolding of a mysterious inner process. "Whoever is in Christ is a new creation" we are assured in Second Corinthians 5:17. We ourselves contain the seed of a future that defies the past, a potential we cannot imagine. Sometimes it helps when sticky situations aren't resolved and success isn't forthcoming, to think of ourselves as tiny black seeds, resting in God's moist palm.

When we clear the tangle of old, dead growth, we model God's promise: "the old things have passed away; behold, new things have come." When we scatter seed on the ground, we image God's action: "See, I am doing something new! Now it springs forth, do you not perceive it?" (Is 43:19, NAB).

Stabilizers

When I first read about the monastic vow of stability, it seemed impossibly distant and removed from my reality. A vow to spend the rest of one's life in the same place seemed incomprehensible to one who collects frequent flier miles as devoutly as some collect china. I couldn't imagine not seeing the ocean again, or the Great Smokies, or the Golden Gate, or the Mississippi.

But as Paul Wilkes interprets the blessing of stability for any Christian life, it's a simple matter of "be here now"—wherever we are.[32] Thich Nhat Hanh's similar encouragement to be present to the moment is indeed a healthy antidote to the constant flux of life in this century. In our toss-away Kleenex culture such an attitude helps us enter the depth of every experience. Even those who do not live within monastery walls can maintain an "interior cloister," that holiest of places where God's peace wells within.[33]

With that background, I began to translate the theory into concrete terms. I thought about the "stabilizers" in my life, functioning like the keel that holds a sailboat steady. It is true that I relish a new dress or recipe, travel frequently, grow bored with routine, and yawn through long speeches. But at the same time, I have been married to the same man for thirty years, have lived in the same house and written at the same desk for twenty, and have changed careers only once.

With those pillars in place, I can appreciate the smaller stabilizers too, like a pale blue robe purchased when my older daughter was one (she is now twenty-five). Without certain books on my shelves, I would be woefully unanchored. The wisdom of Thomas Merton,

Mary Oliver, Kathleen Norris, T. S. Eliot, Annie Dillard, Willa Cather, Flannery O'Connor, Joyce Rupp, and Joan Chittister must be close at hand to keep me grounded. And nothing is sweeter to the touch than cotton sheets washed so repeatedly they take on a soft patina.

There's a certain comfort—if little adventure—in the same patio, surrounded by the same trees and flowers every summer, the same vacation spot like an annual refrain, even the same wooden toilet seat at 3:30 in the morning. (While that may seem odd, it's an improvement over the traveler's chronic complaint: waking in the middle of the night and not knowing what city she's in!) One writer comments: "If we can only see or experience something once, we will live a very watery soup of a life. If we can live it over and over, we will live a rich broth."[34]

If such little familiarities steady the adult psyche, they must be important for the growing psyches of children as well. Teachers report the discombobulation of students who keep sets of clothing at both mom's and dad's houses, and often forget which one has the math book. Not that this is strictly a problem for children of divorced or single parents. A family as extended as E. E. Milne's "Rabbit's friends and relations" cannot prevent kids' shoes from disappearing just as the family is trying to walk out the door. Many children seem to share their parents' sense of fragmentation, and a sensitive toddler will sometimes slip away from the chaos of Christmas or birthday to the security of a little tent beneath the table, or the quiet of a nest beneath the bed.

While most parents won't want to get neurotic about this, and will need to clean out cupboards often, there is something reassuring about the bowl we *always* use for popcorn, the story we *always* read before bed, the cake we *always* have for birthdays, or the routine we follow *every* Fourth of July. The predictable sameness balances a world in which our computers are outdated before we buy them. It implies a healthy ritual, a "thus have we always done it" approach which will probably be modified and altered over the years, but will still provide the reservoir for story and memory.

When the overwhelming possibilities for newness and choice can paralyze us, many people opt for simpler living. If there is only one popcorn bowl, anyone can grab it quickly, because we aren't caught in the weight of the Momentous Decision. Most of us have enough decisions as it is, and snuggle with relief into the same sloppy T-shirt we wear (almost) *every* Saturday or the weathered boots we *always* hike in.

Such reliance on the tried and true must frustrate the folks who specialize in consumer hype. They would be quick to point out that a new car has forty-seven improvements, not understanding how long it's taken us to master the thirty-four gizmos of the old one. We don't need to be driven by artificially created need; it is possible to be happy with old stuff.

I'll admit to being as refreshed by a little retail therapy as any dedicated shopper. But the stabilizers provide a security that enables me to burrow deeper into the larger experiences and opportunities life presents. These objects do not call much attention to themselves; they do not require intensive maintenance or a user's guide. Like all good pointers, they allow me to look beyond them. Only then can I learn what all the great spiritual teachers have taught, "being here, now, is as perfect an act as one can hope to perform."[35]

Notes

Introduction

1. Murray Bodo in Thomas Grady and Paula Huston, eds., *Signatures of Grace* (New York: Dutton, 2000), 189.

2. Susan Ross, *Extravagant Affections* (New York: Continuum, 1998), 117.

3. Joseph Martos, *Doors to the Sacred* (Liguori, MO: Triumph Books, 1991), 5.

4. Ibid., 4.

5. Ross, 77.

6. Ibid., 40, 213.

7. Foreword to Monika Hellwig, *The Meaning of the Sacraments* (Dayton, OH: Pflaum Press, 1981), vii-viii.

Part One

1. Robert Hamma, *Landscapes of the Soul: A Spirituality of Place* (Notre Dame, IN: Ave Maria Press, 1999), 86.

2. Belden Lane, *The Solace of Fierce Landscapes* (New York: Oxford University Press, 1998), 100.

3. Thomas Merton, *Conjectures of a Guilty Bystander* (Garden City, NY: Doubleday Image, 1968), 179.

4. Rumi in Stephen Mitchell, ed., *The Englightened Heart* (New York: HarperCollins, 1989), 59.

5. Quoted in Lane, 54.

6. Henri Nouwen, *Jesus: A Gospel*, ed. Michael O'Loughlin (Maryknoll, NY: Orbis Books, 2001), 36.

7. J. D. Salinger, *Raise High the Roof Beam, Carpenters and Seymour: An Introduction* (New York: Bantam, 1965), 213.

8. Quoted in Lane, 45.

9. Lane, 100.

10. Ibid., 145.

11. Wayne Muller, *Sabbath* (New York: Bantam, 1999), 42, 78.

12. Ibid., 79.

13. Lane, 132.

14. Ibid., 133.

15. Mary Oliver, *House of Light* (Boston: Beacon Press, 1990), 33.

16. Ilene Beckerman, *Mother of the Bride* (Chapel Hill: Algonquin Books, 2000), quoted in *The Denver Post*, July 13, 2002, 10E.

17. Thomas Grady and Paula Huston, eds., *Signatures of Grace* (New York: Dutton, 2000), xi.

18. Ibid., 25.

19. Beatrice Bruteau, *The Easter Mysteries* (New York: Crossroad, 1995), 142.

20. James Dunning, *Echoing God's Word* (Arlington, VA: North American Forum on the Catechumenate, 1993), 358.

21. Quoted in Jan Michael Joncas, "Approaches to Initiation Preaching from Ancient Christian Preachers," *Catechumenate*, January 2000, 16-17.

22. Quoted in Carol Flinders, *The New Laurel's Kitchen* (Berkeley: Ten Speed Press, 1986), 19.

23. Flinders, 20.

24. Ibid., 33.

25. Andrew Greeley, *The Catholic Imagination* (Berkeley: University of California Press, 2000), 39.

26. Ibid., 31.

27. Ibid., 91.

28. Ibid., 96.

29. Mary Oliver, *Winter Hours* (Boston: Houghton Mifflin, 1999), 109.

30. Quoted in Peter Hassrick, ed., *The Georgia O'Keeffe Museum* (New York: Harry Abrams, 1997), 37.

31. Quoted in Sharyn Udall, *O'Keeffe and Texas* (San Antonio: Marion Koogler McNay Art Museum, 1998), 77.

32. Thomas Merton, *The Seven Storey Mountain* (New York: Harcourt Brace, 1978), 37.

33. Mary Pipher, *The Shelter of Each Other* (New York: Ballantine, 1996), 234.

34. Christine Bochen, ed., *Learning to Love: The Journals of Thomas Merton* (New York: HarperCollins, 1998), 54.

35. Ibid., 312.

36. Ibid., 55.

37. Ibid., 317.

38. Ibid., 307.

39. John Steinbeck, *Cannery Row* (New York: Penguin, 1992 edition), 1.

40. John O'Donohue, *Eternal Echoes* (New York: HarperCollins, 1999), 14.

41. Joyce Rupp, *The Cosmic Dance* (Maryknoll, NY: Orbis, 2002), 54.

Part Two

1. Seamus Heaney, "The Fragment," *Electric Light* (New York: Farrar, Straus and Giroux, 2001), 70.

2. Adapted with permission from *St. Anthony Messenger*.

3. Paula Huston, "Matrimony," in Paula Huston and Thomas Grady, eds., *Signatures of Grace* (New York: Dutton, 2000), 159.

4. Murray Bodo, "Holy Orders," in Grady and Huston, *Signatures of Grace*, 166.

5. Paige Byrne Shortal, "Plea for Vocations Is Like Praying for Rain in a Deluge," *National Catholic Reporter*, February 22, 2002, 37.

6. Mike Daley, "Blessings from Unlikely People," *National Catholic Reporter*, February 22, 2002, 2.

7. Rumi, *The Essential Rumi*, trans. Coleman Barks with John Moyne (New York: HarperSanFrancisco, 1995), 6.

8. Hippolytus of Rome, quoted in *The Macmillan Book of Earliest Christian Hymns* (New York: Macmillan, 1988), 68.

9. Quoted in Esther de Waal, *A Seven Day Journey with Thomas Merton* (Ann Arbor, MI: Servant Publications, 1992), 17-18.

10. Bernard Cooke, *Sacraments and Sacramentality* (Mystic, CT: Twenty-Third Publications, 1985), 64.

11. Ibid., 115.

12. John O'Donohue, *Eternal Echoes* (New York: HarperCollins, 1999), 258.

13. Ibid.

14. Adapted with permission from *America* magazine.

15. Mary Pipher, *The Shelter of Each Other* (New York: Ballantine, 1996), 243.

16. Graham Greene, *The End of the Affair* (London: Penguin Books, 1951), 109, 111.

17. Ibid., 112.

18. Ibid., 190.

19. Ibid., 172.

20. Ibid., 131.

21. Graham Greene, *The Power and the Glory* (New York: Viking, 1965), 160.

22. Ibid., 82.

23. Ibid., 284.

24. Ibid., 298.

Part Three

1. Susan Ross, *Extravagant Affections* (New York: Continuum, 1998), 226.

2. Andre Dubus, *Meditations from a Movable Chair* (New York: Knopf, 1998), 89-90.

3. Ross, 42.

4. Quoted by Carol Flinders, "The Work at Hand," in *The New Laurel's Kitchen* (Berkeley: Ten Speed Press, 1986), 28.

5. Flinders, 30.

6. Ibid., 30.

7. Kathleen Norris, "Introduction: Stories Around a Fire," in *The Best American Essays 2001* (Boston: Houghton Mifflin, 2001), xvi.

8. Quoted in Esther de Waal, *A Seven Day Journey with Thomas Merton* (Ann Arbor, MI: Servant Publications, 1992), 20.

9. Brian Doyle, "Give It a Rest," *U.S Catholic*, September 2001, 26-27.

10. Rumi, "Don't grieve. Anything you lose comes round," in Stephen Mitchell, ed., *The Enlightened Heart* (New York: HarperCollins, 1989), 51.

11. Bill Bryson, *A Walk in the Woods* (New York: Broadway Books, 1998), 200.

12. Ibid.

13. Richard Rohr, "We Should Ask Why Few Transformations Happen in Church," *National Catholic Reporter*, February 22, 2002, 8.

14. Ann Schreckenberger, "Clothe Her in Your Care," *U.S. Catholic*, August 2001, 30-31.

15. de Waal, 82.

16. Rich Heffern, "Thomas Berry," *National Catholic Reporter*, August 10, 2001, 4.

17. Ignatius Loyola, "Suscipe," in Michael Harter, ed., *Hearts on Fire: Praying with Jesuits* (St. Louis: Institute of Jesuit Sources, 1993), 84.

18. Beatrice Bruteau, *The Easter Mysteries* (New York: Crossroad, 1995), 144.

19. Seamus Heaney, "Summer Home," in *Opened Ground: Selected Poems, 1966-1996* (New York: Farrar, Straus and Giroux, 1998), 67.

20. Donna Schaper, *Sabbath Keeping* (Cambridge: Cowley Publications, 1999) 87.

21. Ross, 72.

22. Ibid., 77.

23. Frederick Buechner, *Wishful Thinking: A Theological ABC* (New York: Harper & Row, 1973), 82.

24. Kathleen Norris, *Amazing Grace* (New York: Riverhead Books, 1998), 151.

25. Gerard Manley Hopkins, "The Leaden Echo and the Golden Echo," in *Poems and Prose of Gerard Manley Hopkins* (Baltimore: Penguin Books, 1956), 54.

26. Bruteau, 182.

Part Four

1. Mary Oliver, *Winter Hours* (Boston: Houghton Mifflin, 1999), 98, 100.

2. Andrew Greeley, *The Catholic Imagination* (Berkeley: University of California Press, 2000), 153.

3. Raymond Brown, *The Gospel According to John*, i-xii (Garden City, NY: Doubleday, 1966), LXXIV.

4. Ibid., LXXII.

5. Ibid., LXXVIII.

6. bid., 275.

7. John Tieman, "All I Will Ever Need," *America*, September 17, 1999, 20.

8. Brown, 397.

9. Ibid., 671.

10. Adapted with permission from *Ligouri* magazine.

11. Beatrice Bruteau, *The Easter Mysteries* (New York: Crossroad, 1995), 165.

12. Bernard Cooke, *Sacraments and Sacramentality* (Mystic, CT: Twenty-Third Publications, 1985), 119.

13. Quoted from *Carmina Gadelica* in Esther de Waal, *The Celtic Way of Prayer* (New York: Doubleday, 1997), 29.

14. Bruteau, 183.

15. Joyce Rupp, *Inviting God In* (Notre Dame, IN: Ave Maria Press, 2001), 44.

16. Quoted in Thomas Grady and Paula Huston, eds., *Signatures of Grace* (New York: Dutton, 2000), 202.

17. Ibid., 189.

18. Thomas Moore, *Original Self* (New York: HarperCollins, 2000), 22.

19. Mircea Eliade, *Images and Symbols: Studies in Religious Symbolism* (Princeton, NJ: Princeton University Press, 1991), 55-56.

20. Moore, 75.

21. Eliade, 12.

22. de Waal, 60.

23. Ibid., 36.

24. Ibid.

25. Ibid., 70.

26. Ibid., 83.

27. Ibid., 17.

28. Eliade, 33.

29. Barbara Bedway, "Bridges to God," in E. Lee Hancock, ed., *The Book of Women's Sermons* (New York: Riverhead Books, 1999), 41.

30. Cate Terwilliger, "Expanded Moments in Garden," *The Denver Post*, May 23, 2001, 6E.

31. Bedway, 41.

32. Paul Wilkes, *Beyond the Walls: Monastic Wisdom for Everyday Life* (New York: Doubleday, 1999), 68.

33. Ibid., 70.

34. Donna Schaper, *Sabbath Keeping* (Cambridge, MA: Cowley Publications, 1999), 52-53.

35. Wilkes, 78.

Bibliography

Beckerman, Ilene. *Mother of the Bride*. Chapel Hill: Algonquin Books, 2000.

Bochen, Christine, ed. *Learning to Love: The Journals of Thomas Merton*. New York: HarperCollins, 1998.

Brown, Raymond. *The Gospel According to John*. Garden City, NY: Doubleday, 1966.

Bruteau, Beatrice. *The Easter Mysteries*. New York: Crossroad, 1995.

Bryson, Bill. *A Walk in the Woods*. New York: Broadway Books, 1998.

Buechner, Frederick. *Wishful Thinking: A Theological ABC*. New York: Harper & Row, 1973.

Cooke, Bernard. *Sacraments and Sacramentality*. Mystic, CT: Twenty-Third Publications, 1985.

Daley, Mike. "Blessings from Unlikely People," *National Catholic Reporter*, February 22, 2002.

De Waal, Esther. *The Celtic Way of Prayer*. New York: Doubleday, 1997.

_____. *A Seven Day Journey with Thomas Merton*. Ann Arbor, MI: Servant Publications, 1992.

Doyle, Brian. "Give It a Rest," *U.S. Catholic*, September 2001.

Dubus, Andre. *Meditations from a Movable Chair*. New York: Knopf, 1998.

Dunning, James. *Echoing God's Word*. Arlington, VA: North American Forum on the Catechumenate, 1993.

Eliade, Mircea. *Images and Symbols: Studies in Religious Symbolism*. Princeton, NJ: Princeton University Press, 1991.

Flinders, Carol. *The New Laurel's Kitchen*. Berkeley: Ten Speed Press, 1986.

Grady, Thomas and Paula Huston, eds. *Signatures of Grace*. New York: Dutton, 2000.

Greeley, Andrew. *The Catholic Imagination*. Berkeley: University of California Press, 2000.

Greene, Graham. *The End of the Affair*. London: Penguin Books, 1951.

_____. *The Power and the Glory*. New York: Viking, 1965.

Hamma, Robert. *Landscapes of the Soul: A Spirituality of Place*. Notre Dame, IN: Ave Maria Press, 1999.

Hancock, E. Lee, ed. *The Book of Women's Sermons*. New York: Riverhead Books, 1999.

Harter, Michael, ed. *Hearts on Fire: Praying with Jesuits*. St. Louis: Institute of Jesuit Sources, 1993.

Hassrick, Peter, ed. *The Georgia O'Keeffe Museum*. New York: Harry Abrams, 1997.

Heaney, Seamus. *Electric Light*. New York: Farrar, Straus and Giroux, 2001.

_____. *Opened Ground: Selected Poems, 1966-1996*. New York: Farrar, Straus and Giroux, 1998.

Heffern, Rich. "Thomas Berry," *National Catholic Reporter*, August 10, 2001.

Hellwig, Monika. *The Meaning of the Sacraments*. Dayton, OH: Pflaum Press, 1981.

Hopkins, Gerard Manley. *Poems and Prose of Gerard Manley Hopkins*. Baltimore: Penguin Books, 1956.

Joncas, Jan Michael. "Approaches to Initiation Preaching from Ancient Christian Preachers," *Catechumenate*, January 2000.

Lane, Belden. *The Solace of Fierce Landscapes*. New York: Oxford University Press, 1998.

Martos, Joseph. *Doors to the Sacred*. Liguori, MO: Triumph Books, 1991.

Merton, Thomas. *Conjectures of a Guilty Bystander*. Garden City, NY: Doubleday Image, 1968.

_____. *The Seven Storey Mountain*. New York: Harcourt Brace, 1978.

Mitchell, Stephen, ed. *The Enlightened Heart*. New York: HarperCollins, 1989.

Moore, Thomas. *Original Self*. New York: HarperCollins, 2000.

Muller, Wayne. *Sabbath*. New York: Bantam, 1999.

Norris, Kathleen. *Amazing Grace*. New York: Riverhead Books, 1998.

_____. "Introduction: Stories Around a Fire," in *The Best American Essays 2001*. Boston: Houghton Mifflin, 2001.

Nouwen, Henri. *Jesus: A Gospel*, ed. Michael O'Loughlin. Maryknoll, NY: Orbis Books, 2001.

O'Donohue, John. *Eternal Echoes*. New York: HarperCollins, 1999.

Oliver, Mary. *House of Light*. Boston: Beacon Press, 1990.

_____. *Winter Hours*. Boston: Houghton Mifflin, 1999.

Pipher, Mary. *The Shelter of Each Other*. New York: Ballantine, 1996.

Rohr, Richard. "We Should Ask Why Few Transformations Happen in Church," *National Catholic Reporter*, February 22, 2002.

Ross, Susan. *Extravagant Affections*. New York: Continuum, 1998.

Rumi, *The Essential Rumi*, trans. Coleman Barks with John Moyne. New York: HarperSanFrancisco, 1995.

Rupp, Joyce. *The Cosmic Dance*. Maryknoll, NY: Orbis, 2002.

_____. *Inviting God In*. Notre Dame, IN: Ave Maria Press, 2001.

Salinger, J. D. *Raise High the Roof Beam, Carpenters and Seymour: An Introduction*. New York: Bantam, 1965.

Schaper, Donna. *Sabbath Keeping*. Cambridge: Cowley Publications, 1999.

Shortal, Paige. "Plea for Vocations Is Like Praying for Rain in a Deluge," *National Catholic Reporter*, February 22, 2002.

Shreckenberger, Ann. "Clothe Her in Your Care," *U.S. Catholic*, August 2001.

Steinbeck, John. *Cannery Row*. New York: Penguin, 1992.

Terwilliger, Cate. "Expanded Moments in Garden," *The Denver Post*, May 23, 2001.

Tieman, John. "All I Will Ever Need," *America*, September 17, 1999.

Udall, Sharyn. *O'Keeffe and Texas*. San Antonio: Marion Koogler McNay Art Museum, 1998.

Wilkes, Paul. *Beyond the Walls: Monastic Wisdom for Everyday Life*. New York: Doubleday, 1999.

Kathy Coffey is an editor and a frequent speaker at workshops around the country. She is an award-winning author of numerous articles and several books, including *Hidden Women of the Gospels, God in the Moment, Dancing in the Margins,* and *God Knows Parenting Is a Wild Ride.* Coffey lives with her family in Denver, Colorado.